D. L. MOODY

D. L. MOODY

A WORKER IN SOULS

BY

GAMALIEL BRADFORD

 BOOKS FOR LIBRARIES PRESS
FREEPORT, NEW YORK

First Published 1927
Reprinted 1972

269.2
B72d
88572
april 1974

Library of Congress Cataloging in Publication Data

Bradford, Gamaliel, 1863-1932.
    D. L. Moody; a worker in souls.

    ([BCL/select bibliographies reprint series])
    Reprint of the 1927 ed.
    Bibliography: p.
    1.   Moody, Dwight Lyman, 1837-1899.
BV3785.M7B7   1972   269'.2'0924 [B]   72-1275
ISBN 0-8369-6821-2

PRINTED IN THE UNITED STATES OF AMERICA

TO

THE MEMORY OF

HARRIET FORD CUTLER

Nil magnum, nil altum, nil gratum, nil acceptum tibi sit, nisi pure Deus, aut de Deo sit.—IMITÀTION OF CHRIST.

Il faut être assez profondément sceptique pour paraître quelquefois Chrétien.—SAINTE-BEUVE.

Moi, je crois à tout; je suis sceptique.—FRENCH COMEDY.

CONTENTS

CONTENTS

ILLUSTRATIONS

D. L. MOODY:
A WORKER IN SOULS

CHRONOLOGY

DWIGHT LYMAN MOODY

Born, Northfield, Massachusetts, February 5, 1837.
Entered shoe business in Boston, 1854.
Joined Mount Vernon Street Congregational Church, 1856.
Went to Chicago, 1856.
Gave up business for religious work, 1861.
Married Emma C. Revell, 1862.
Established Chicago church, 1863.
Met Sankey, 1870.
Revival in British Isles, 1873-1875.
Revivals in large American cities, 1875-1877.
Northfield Seminary established, 1879.
Mount Hermon School established, 1881.
Second British mission, 1881-1884.
Chicago Bible Institute established, 1887.
Northfield conferences established, 1887.
Last revival in Kansas City, 1899.
Died, Northfield, December 22, 1899.
Ira David Sankey, born August 28, 1840, died August 13, 1908.

D. L. MOODY:
A WORKER IN SOULS

CHAPTER I

THE GROWTH OF A SOUL

I

WHEN one looks upon the ease and richness and abundance of modern American life, its kaleidoscopic color and variety, its mad bustle and profusion of motion and locomotion, one feels more inclined to descant upon its possessions than upon its needs. Yet if one stops in all the hurry to reflect, the needs become apparent and crying, and in all the loud hurly-burly not one need stands out more patent than the need of God. The world has always needed Him no doubt. But it seems as if the America of to-day needed Him most because it is so complacently satisfied to get along without Him. Oh, we have churches enough, priests enough, sermons enough, charities and good works enough, or at any rate abounding. But they all seem ingeniously contrived to cover the void. For divers reasons, some of which will develop later, God seems to have drifted far away from most of us, or we from Him, so far that neither airplane nor wireless will suffice to call Him back. Now a generation ago D. L. Moody was an immense, magnificent agency for bringing men to God. You may not sympathize with all of his methods, you may even feel that in some cases they defeated their object; but you cannot deny that he worked in his own way with a tremendous, tireless zeal to supply the greatest need of his country and of the world, and for that reason the study of his methods, his purposes, his results, and of his personal character, must always have a profound interest. As to the need we have his own testimony: "I do not know of anything that America needs more to-day than men and women on fire with the fire of heaven." [1] As to the zeal and the effort we have the admirable statement of Mr. Duffus: "In his rage to save souls he traveled more than a million miles, addressed more than a hundred million people, and personally prayed and pleaded with seven hundred and fifty thousand sinners. All in all, it is very probable, as his admirers claim, that he reduced the population of hell by a million souls." [2]

Dwight Lyman Moody was born in Northfield,

Massachusetts, in 1837. The three names are sufficient to show the Anglo-Saxon stock, and the man typified that stock in all respects, so much so that he was almost as much at home in England as in America. His father, who was a mason, died when the boy was very small, and the mother brought up a large family with patience, devotion, and self-sacrifice. Dwight knocked about the New England country town as a child. As a youth he went to Boston, and after some struggles settled into his uncle's business of shoe-selling. He was a vigorous and aggressive salesman. In 1856 he became a member of the Mount Vernon Street Church. The business of working for God attracted him at once, but Boston did not wholly suit him. He drifted out to Chicago and there began both to sell shoes and to save sinners. But the latter occupation was more congenial and he soon gave himself up to it wholly. In 1862 he married a noble woman who was always of incalculable help to him. He reached out first for poor boys, then for poor men, then for poor and rich alike. During the Civil War, though not in the army, he did active missionary work among the soldiers. Though he was never ordained as a minister, he for a time carried on a church in Chicago, and carried it on with his usual fierce energy and success. He met Sankey, and at once saw how he could employ him. Then two brief visits to Europe confirmed his instinct for larger usefulness, and in 1873 he and Sankey started on the two-year tour of the British Isles which founded their world reputation as evangelists. Returning to his own country, he continued the work everywhere with equal success, and though in later years the element of direct preaching gradually diminished in proportion to that of religious and educational organization, he was until his death in Northfield in 1899 essentially an exhorter and teacher. It is difficult to think of him as anything else, the more so as he entered into his work with such immense, exuberant relish. He enjoyed it with an enjoyment all the more keen for being righteous and divinely authorized. He could have said of himself, as Frances Willard did, "The chief wonder of my life is that I dare to have so good a time, both physically, mentally, and religiously." [3]

To understand Moody we have to keep before us always the New England background. There was the rough, hard, simple life, energetic, upright, conscientious if on somewhat conventional lines, but wholly unillumined, without color or charm. There was always the atmosphere of religion, at once stimulating and stifling. In Moody's case the religion happened to be nominally Unitarian, and therefore his doctrinal basis had to be established later. But the Unitarianism of that day, especially in such types as Moody's pastor and mother, was far more orthodox than the orthodoxy of this, and the religious tone about the boy was not very unlike what the man carried to his grave. Underlying it all was the New England landscape, that varied and haunting beauty of rolling hills with their spring and autumn splendor, of rocky pastures, spread wide with juniper and berry bushes, of great elm-besprinkled meadows stretching beside the Connecticut, and best of all the river itself, flowing forever, like human life, out of mystery into mystery. Even if his boyhood was not very conscious of these things, they got hold of Moody and kept hold of him all his days. He liked to wander, would not have been happy to do anything else; but from all the wandering he returned again and again to Northfield with an infinite sense of satisfaction and content.

D. L. MOODY: A WORKER IN SOULS

II

A good deal is told us about Moody's early
years, but it is more extensive than definite. Perhaps the most striking fact is the lack of a father's
control in the training of such a temperament.
The mother gave love and won it eminently. But
she could not maintain the sterner discipline, and
the boy's wayward, violent spirit sorely needed it.
The mother herself said of him, "He used to think
himself a man when he was only a boy." [4] One
who had exactly the reverse experience, being
brought up without a mother, by a father much of
Moody's type, can well divine how it would work.

Without being ever in the least egotistical,
Moody was always contriving to bring hints and
suggestions of his early life into his sermons, and
they are therefore a rich source of biographical
information. It is evident that, like other boys,
he disliked manual labor. "When I was a boy,"
he says, "I used, among other things, to hoe the
corn on a farm; and I used to hoe it so badly, in
order to get over so much ground, that at night I
had to put down a stick in the ground, so as to
know next morning where I had left off." [5] Probably he liked play better than work, but we get
very little insight into any of the boyish amuse-

BIRTHPLACE OF DWIGHT L. MOODY AT NORTHFIELD, MASS.

D. L. MOODY'S GRANDMOTHER.

From a portrait taken in 1856.

D. L. MOODY'S MOTHER.

From a portrait taken in 1856.

ments. He is said to have been a good runner, and he was quick and active even after his weight increased, but there is no mention of swimming, or of skating, or of sliding on those tempting hills, no suggestion of games or contests. New England boys have always had these things in some shape and it seems likely that Moody's energy and vigor would have shone in them. They might have afforded moral lessons, also; but I have not found that he drew them. He did have all his life a fondness for the rather crude form of humor called practical jokes, and in this as in some other things, he much resembled his distinguished contemporary, P. T. Barnum, though Barnum's calling in life was slightly more conducive to indulgence in such diversion. To post a notice of a temperance lecture and draw a crowd for nothing, to startle a farmer's horses, just as he was taking a drink, and tip him back into his wagon, to have a cat jump out of Cæsar's coffin when the oration of Antony was being delivered over it, such incidents were a great relief in the monotonous life of a country boy.

Of boyhood friends and associates there is little record in Moody's later years. There may have been such things, but he does not allude to them.

He sometimes refers to men whom he knew as boys, but there is no sign of particular intimacy, and of girls there is no suggestion at all. On the other hand, he seems to have been devoted to his family, perhaps in part because he left them fairly early. He speaks with profound emotion of the brother who disappeared for years and the death of his younger brother Samuel caused him bitter sorrow. Of his mother he always speaks with reverence and tenderness. She did not indeed spare old-fashioned severity, and the boy probably needed it. Once when she was whipping him, he remarked that it did not hurt, whereupon she saw to it that it did.[6] But her tenderness, her devotion, her wisdom, made a lasting impression, and until her death he reverted to her for counsel and comfort.

There are numerous references in his sermons to the religious experience of childhood; but they are usually for edification, either positively or negatively, and therefore cannot be entirely relied upon. He tells us that he detested Sunday.[7] He tells us that sermons bored him, and he made up his mind that he would avoid them when he could.[8] He was of course brought up to prayer, but in childhood he looked mainly to its practical efficacy, as indeed he was inclined to all his life. A heavy fence rail once fell upon him, and he could not possibly lift it. He prayed to God to help him and then he lifted the rail quite easily.[9] Death and its terrors often haunted him. He would stand beside a grave and think of its ghastliness.[10] When the funeral bell tolled out the age of the departed, he thought how it might some day toll for him. "I felt terribly afraid when I thought of the cold hand of death feeling for the cords of life, and being launched into eternity, to go to an unknown world." [11] All this to emphasize that from such terrors in later life he was superbly free.

III

The most interesting thing about Moody's boyhood was his education, or lack of it. He did not like study or his books and avoided them when he could. He tells us that a teacher who worked by love could do more than one who punished.[12] And it is said that he learned for love of his mother, but for nothing else. But I imagine that love affected the intention more than the act. A story is told by one of his critics which may not be true, but is to the point. In later years he met a man and assailed him with the usual question,

"Are you a Christian?" "I am a Unitarian," was the answer. "Then you are not a Christian. I was a Unitarian until I was seventeen when I left Northfield and I know." But the man replied: "I was your teacher in Northfield. You left there before you were seventeen, and you did not know enough to be a Unitarian." [13] Other evidence, including Moody's own, amply supports this lack of even rudimentary book-learning. What is more important is that he not only lacked education, but that at times—by no means always—he expressed a contempt for it: "We are a bad lot; and what you want is to tell men so—not flatter them, and tell them how angelic they are because they have some education. An educated rascal is the meanest kind of a rascal." [14]

Which of course does not imply that he had not the most acute, quick, versatile, and penetrating intelligence. No man could surpass him in keen Yankee shrewdness, applied at all times and to all sorts of things. You could not over-reach him in a bargain, you could not deceive him in a man's character, unless he was willing to be deceived. He kept up with the movement of the world and with current events. He read the newspapers, though perhaps chiefly to find illustrations for his sermons. He watched men's faces and used them to sound men's hearts, and his opportunities for doing this have rarely been surpassed: "He had unquestionably looked into the countenances of more people than any man who ever lived (100,000,000 Arthur T. Pierson estimates), and had made the personal acquaintance of more individuals than many of us have ever seen. And yet he seemed never to forget any of those who had once made a distinct and positive impression upon his mind." [15]

The education of life was there in large measure, at least of life viewed in certain aspects. But the education of life, even at its best, needs to be supplemented by books and thought, and such supplementing was not in Moody's line. General reading he never at any time knew much about. It is true that in his sermons there is an occasional historical allusion which surprises, until you realize how easily it might have been gathered into that retentive memory. But of reading for the pleasure or even the profit of it there is no sign. History, philosophy, science, poetry in themselves did not exist for him. Novels he abhorred: "I could not read those flashy novels. I have no taste for them, no desire to read them; but if I did I would not do it." [16] Yet novels, while perhaps morally dissipating, are intellectually profitable far beyond what most people believe.

Nor did Moody do much at any time in his life in the way of abstract reflection. In his terse, flashing way he once remarked: "There is hope for a man when once he begins to think." [17] Sometimes the weary reader of his thousands of pages wishes that he could ever have begun. He was so busy, so rushed, so driven in saving souls that quiet, thoughtful, intense reflection, for itself, was something he had no time for. "A careful self-analysis was unnatural if not impossible throughout his entire life," says one of his most acute and sympathetic critics. [18] He himself deprecates and deplores anything of the kind. No doubt self-dissection has its dangers. But he at least was not greatly exposed to them, and his biographer is occasionally forced to regret that he did not indulge in self-dissection a little more freely. To attack the great knotty problems of the world by cool, careful, dispassionate logic was not his method. He wanted to cut them, to tear them out of his way, to dissipate them and crush them and forget them.

Not that he was not capable of intellectual concentration, when he felt that it was required. On the contrary, even in later life he was a most ardent and passionate student. When he was at home in Northfield, he would rise at four o'clock and shut himself up to work for a long time before breakfast. Also, he met many educated men, and he had the gift of genius for using the work of others. He had assistants who read for him and called his attention to passages he ought to see. But this intellectual effort was—shall I say fatally?— concentrated upon one thing, the Bible, and in youth and age he was little disposed to go outside of it. A friend says of his earlier years that he did not know of Moody's owning any other book but a copy of the New Testament.[19] The same friend said to him a little later: "Moody, if you want to draw wine out of a cask, it is needful first to put some in. You are all the time talking, and you ought to begin to study."[20] The young preacher was willing, anxious; but his mind was intensive, not extensive in its working: it wanted to find and hold one clue to the whole world. To be sure, it is said that he developed, that all his life he was learning and growing, and this is true. A spirit so naturally vital and progressive could not help growing. He reached out, he grasped, he seized from everywhere, but always the things that bore in the direction he wished. It is said that his later sermons were much in advance of the earlier, in finish and in breadth. This I have been unable to discover, perhaps because the sermons as printed have been subjected to industrious editing.

In any case the intellectual deficiencies were there and cannot be overlooked. He himself was not disposed to overlook them: "One great torment of his soul was the thought that he was an ignorant man, and yet was looked upon as a religious teacher," says one of his biographers.[21] Perhaps this is slightly exaggerated; but there is no doubt that he was sensitive on the subject, and more than sensitive, deeply regretful that anything should hamper his work for the Lord. Yet here, as always, in Rosalind's charming phrase, you could not take him without his answer. When a sympathetic critic once pointed out that the only drawback to his sermons was his imperfect knowledge of grammar and English, Moody replied that he knew and deplored this as much as any one. "But," he added, "I am doing all I can for God with the gifts I have. Are you?"

THE GROWTH OF A SOUL

IV

It is well to pause and examine more fully Moody's intellectual and spiritual deficiencies, as they affected and infected the larger significance of his whole career. No doubt similar deficiencies affected the vast mass of humanity which he was so nobly and passionately laboring to save. Still, one wishes that a leader of men had not been quite so much hampered by them.

The superficial weaknesses are evident enough, the slips in grammar, the raw colloquial English and rough-and-ready expression. Much of this was edited out of the printed sermons. Much of it even disappeared in the reports given in the more intelligent newspapers. As originally uttered, the talk often had elements that were trying to cultivated hearers. Moody was well aware of this and did his best to overcome the defects. But the rush and fire and enthusiasm of his main subject swept him beyond minor considerations of correctness, and in most cases they swept away his hearers also. The chief thing to note is the admirable comment of Dr. Goss, which, if not strictly exact, is perfectly characteristic of the man's native genius and power of growth, that he never made the same blunder twice.[22]

These superficial drawbacks, however, are of small consequence. What does matter is the wide world of intellectual and spiritual experience which Moody never knew anything about and never wanted to. One gets so irritated sometimes over the utter absence of the things that seem to some of us to count that one is tempted to ask, of what use is it to save a soul when there is nothing in it worth saving? Against which should be urged, justly, the other point of view, which Moody never fails to emphasize, that all the culture in the world is of no value for a soul which has not the only element that can make it a soul at all. "Culture is all right in its place, but to talk about culture before a man is born of God, before he has received this incorruptible seed into his heart, is the height of madness." [23]

Yet, for example, there is science, the intense passion for pure truth, wherever it may lead, the eager, endless curiosity to probe more and more deeply into the secrets of the universe. Two of the greatest of Moody's contemporaries, Sainte-Beuve and Darwin, are typical of this passion as he is of a passion that is different. Neither Sainte-Beuve nor Darwin cared in the least about saving souls. Neither bothered much about his own soul, except to make it ampler and richer and more fruitful by the endless acquisition of knowledge. Sainte-Beuve's favorite motto was the old Latin saying, "one wearies of everything except to understand." Darwin put it in his quiet, simple, unpretentious fashion: "I believe there exists, and I feel within me, an instinct for truth, or knowledge, or discovery, of something the same nature as the instinct of virtue." [24] The instinct of virtue was enough for Moody, and knowledge, except as subordinate to that, and then in a very minor degree, was infinitely inconsequential. When General Booth visited the British Museum, he prayed that "God would enable me to acquire knowledge to increase my power of usefulness." [25] This is an excellent disposition, surely, but it is far, far from the scientific spirit. It was Moody's disposition at all times, when he was interested in knowledge at all. And he is too often inclined to express a contempt for it. The essence of the scientific spirit is a perpetual, curious questioning, of all things and all men. Moody met millions of men. But he was too eager to pour out himself to have much time to question. He had but the one question, which he plied life with in a thousand forms:

D. L. MOODY: A WORKER IN SOULS

"Are you a Christian?" All other questions were unnecessary.

Again, take art. The beauty, the splendor of esthetic emotion is what most makes life worth living for some of us. It may be sculpture, it may be painting, it may be music, it may be poetry. All of them offer the height of rapture freely to any one who will or can accept of it. All of them were completely lost on Moody. Even poetry he refers to only in the form of hymns, obviously because he thinks they may affect his auditors. The supreme magic of high-wrought expression even of his own supreme interests meant nothing to him. Take the broadest and most human form of esthetic delight, the appreciation of nature. Moody's biographers assert that this appreciation was strong in him and it is evident that the home landscape associated with his childhood always kept a pull on his heart. But his sermons show not the slightest sensibility to the charms of the natural world. Even for his manifold purposes of illustration he makes little use of them. When he wants to deal with birds, he falls back upon the lark and nightingale, because he has seen them mentioned in books. The world in which Thoreau passed his whole existence, the utterly forgetful self-surrender to the magic of birds and flowers and trees and stars, would have been incomprehensible to the prophet of Northfield. These things had no value for saving souls, they had no souls to be saved: why bother with them?

Note that in all these matters it is not the mere ignorance and limitation that are hurtful and dangerous. Ignorance is above all the mark of the age in which we live, and it is the mark of those who are supposed to be learned as much as of any. Within the last two hundred years the possibilities of human knowledge have increased with appalling rapidity. This is in part what Henry Adams means by the somewhat nebulous theory of acceleration which fills the later chapters of his Autobiography. What everybody knows collectively is vastly, infinitely out of proportion to what anybody knows, or can know. The best trained, the most thoroughly educated, simply grope in an obscure mist of what they might find out and ought to find out, and never will. In simple ignorance, therefore, minds of the Moody type differ little from any other. The difference comes, if one may say so, in the knowledge of ignorance, and it is in the firm acquisition of this knowledge that, for the future, must lie the beginning of wisdom. The wise man is conscious of his limits, knows that he knows little or nothing, and his wisdom brings modesty, humility, quiet searching of the heart, freedom from self-assurance, from positiveness, from aggressive dogmatism. Now there is no question but that Moody theoretically proclaimed this humility, admitted that there was much that he did not know and that others did. But the attitude did not take hold of his life. The timidity, the uncertainty, the sceptical conservatism implied in the wisdom indicated above were utterly foreign to his nature. He strode right out into the unknown, with his eye so firmly fixed upon one glorious object, that doubt and tremor and hesitation were forever abandoned. There was but one thing really worth knowing. That thing could be known by any man or woman, any day, even by the humblest and poorest. Why trouble about knowing anything else? He did not trouble, could not wholly repress his contempt for those who did. Now the proposition, "I know the one thing needful to be known," too easily resolves itself into, "What I do not know is not worth knowing."

There is this qualification, however, and it is important. The old saying was, knowledge is power. It is almost equally true, especially in these days, that ignorance is power. The knowledge of ignorance, which we have seen to be the chief ingredient of wisdom, may give tolerance and humility, but it tends to hamper and to cripple in practical life. Men of great, energetic, far-reaching action often succeed as much by their limitations as by their intellectual equipment, as Gaston Boissier has admirably shown in regard to the failures of Cicero. The soldier, the statesman, the man of large affairs, the practical reformer, must certainly have special knowledge for his purposes, but the larger knowledge of ignorance merely restrains him by interfering with quick decision and ready resource. "I would rather have zeal without knowledge; and there is a good deal of knowledge without zeal," said Moody himself.[26] It must frankly be admitted that his magnificent ignorance was a great factor in the furious energy of his attack upon indifference and evil.

V

On this point of ignorance and lack of education it is interesting to compare Moody with some prominent men who have been equally without early advantages or indifferent to them, and have had to make their way in the world, and made it. Among Moody's contemporaries he was often likened to Grant. Grant acted rather than talked, and hence had less occasion to betray his deficiencies. As a critic of the day rather cruelly expressed it: "We observe the resemblance, but we are also impressed with the difference: Grant knows something and says little; Moody knows nothing and talks all the time." [27] But the two had a certain physical resemblance and they were alike in their power over men and their singular gift for making the best of even slight opportunities.

By far the most interesting figure to compare with Moody, is that of Lincoln. Both had the same struggle with narrow means and limited advantages in their youth. Both educated themselves and used powers amounting to the highest genius in benefiting their fellow men, Lincoln for this world, Moody for the next. There is only one meeting recorded between them, when Lincoln visited Moody's Sunday School in Chicago and made some rather perfunctory remarks as to what it might mean to the boys to have such teaching. But one easily imagines the widest possibilities of talk between the two, and one wonders with what depths of tender and sympathetic irony Lincoln would have met the inevitable query, "Are you a Christian?"

As to intellectual and spiritual training, Lincoln, like Moody, was a reverent, an assiduous, a studious reader of the Bible. But Moody said frankly: "I have one rule about books. I do not read any book, unless it will help me to understand *the* book." [28] To the Bible Lincoln added Shakespeare, and one sees at once that here is a vast spiritual difference. Shakespeare sums up all that was outside of Moody's world. I do not find that he read the poet, I do not imagine he ever read him attentively. I have looked for Shakespeare allusions and I have noted but two, an incidental reference to the song in "As You Like It," illustrating ingratitude,[29] and a comparison of the Bible and Shakespeare as literature, greatly to the disadvantage of the latter.[30]

The consideration of Shakespeare in connection with Moody is especially fruitful, because some elements of resemblance between them are so marked. Both began at the bottom of the ladder and made their way up by sheer personal power. Both were without formal education and had the richest faculty for extracting education from life. Both made instinctive, cunning, almost inspired use of words to affect the world enormously. But what a strange difference in their spiritual attitude! To Moody this world was in theory a chaos of putrid horror, to be escaped from and forgotten in the absorbed contemplation of another. To Shakespeare this world was almost enough, at least the passion and the glory and the splendor of it fill his pages sufficiently to make another world for the time dispensable. All men and women he understood and loved, not as they might be, but as they were. It was not only saints that he sought and painted, indeed the saints, from their other-worldliness, get but scant attention. It was not only the pure and noble, it was common souls, torn by passion and struggle, weltering in depths as well as triumphing on heights, but all lovable just because they were human like himself. He turned to Desdemona and Cordelia and Juliet and Cleopatra alike. What place is there in Moody's world for the wit of Mercutio, or for the riotous laughter of Falstaff and Sir Toby Belch? Shakespeare had place and genial welcome for them all.

Especially, there is one figure who to me embodies largely the Shakespearean attitude, and is the most ethereal offspring of the Shakespearean imagination, a figure quite unparalleled in other literary work, or paralleled only to prove Shakespeare's superiority. I mean the clown, Touchstone, or Feste, or the Fool in Lear. Few human beings are more opposite to the type of Moody and more impervious to the Moody efforts at salvation than the Shakespearean fool, and as such I wish to keep him, like a gleaming thread running through all these various chapters. It must be understood at once that this creature of immortal, ideal lightness and grace and sunshine and tenderness, is by no means a fool in the ordinary sense. By some inborn oddity, some strange remoteness of spiritual imperfection, or super-perfection, he simply turns the world topsy-turvy, and makes fleeting thistledown of the deepest passion and thought. As the clown in a modern play, which attempts to reproduce the Shakespearean ideal, expresses it, "Thus ye shall know folly ever; for the weakness of our skulls lies not in mere doltishness, in stone-like ignorance. But we trifle where the wise are sad, and over trifles which make the wise merry we waste the ripe fruit of deliberation. We dally where the world pants eagerly, we toil when the world sleeps. Love, ambition, high contemplation, hungry hope—these are the wise man's passions, they are but dreams to the fool." With endless depths of delicate irony and subtle grace, this airy creature turns into inconsequent evanescence the wide mouthings of statesman and reformer and preacher and philosopher, and puffs them away from him with the light breath of childish melody, such as the ballad-scrap of Feste,

> "When that I was and a little tiny boy,
>   With hey-ho, the wind and the rain,
> A foolish thing was but a toy,
>   For the rain it raineth every day,"

or the bit of world-deep folk-song that delighted Anatole France,

> "Les petites marionettes
>   Font, font, font
> Trois petits tours,
>   Et puis s'en vont."

For clowns and Moodys alike do their three swift, fading turns, and vanish away, the clowns accepting their fate gayly or wistfully, the Moodys fighting it with the best earthly and unearthly weapons they can find or grasp.

VI

And Moody's weapons certainly were not delicate irony and subtle grace. He wanted to make the world over, and he went at it with a hammer.

40

But before he made over the world, he had to be made over himself, or, as it was generally put in his day, perhaps a little less generally at present, he had to be converted. The process is well worth attention; for as Lincoln's Shakespeare has it,

"Out of these convertites
There is much matter to be heard and learned."

The phenomena of conversion have been elaborately and fully studied within recent years by such authorities as James, Starbuck, Coe, Leuba, and many others, especially in their more general and comparative aspects in the volume by Professor Underwood entitled: "Conversion: Christian and Non-Christian." The result of these studies is that, while you may explain the matter very differently according to varying philosophical and theological points of view, the psychological experience of conversion is quite undeniable and is of the utmost spiritual importance. "Conversion," says Professor Underwood, "is not simply a lingering superstition among certain sects, but an undeniable fact, occurring at all periods in the history of the Christian Church." [31]

Of the various not wholly satisfactory definitions of conversion perhaps the best is that of William James, which I should prefer to modify something as follows, to the effect that a soul divided, beaten, baffled by anguish, confusion, and tragic conflict is reduced by the action of some inward power, divine or otherwise, to unity and peace. Professor Underwood has amply shown the manifestations of this process in other religions besides Christianity, in Buddhism, in Hebraism, in Mohammedanism. Extensive investigations have been made by Starbuck, Coe, and others as to the age when conversion is most apt to take place, and there seems no question that this is the period of adolescence and is more or less contemporary with sexual development, but the best authorities, like James, strenuously resist the attempt to identify the religious transformation entirely with the sexual. The differences between the attitudes of the two sexes toward conversion have also been tabulated in a most interesting if not always very conclusive manner.

Another curious point is, how far conversion is necessarily a gradual process. That it often appears to occur with overwhelming suddenness is beyond doubt; but the explanation of this, in most cases, would seem to be that an intense and prolonged inhibition, repression, and resistance, of the nature so dear to the Freudians, finally gives way under some touch of casual association or divine influence, whichever you please, and the repressed impulse sweeps all barriers before it in a flood of relief and ecstasy.

The actual emotional experiences attending conversion have been recorded and analyzed by innumerable subjects in all ages, with extraordinary vividness and power. A more or less prolonged agony of doubt, or distress, or question, or fear usually precedes, and I do not know how a brief extract can illustrate this more forcibly than does the account given by the evangelist Finney of one of his subjects: "Accustomed as I was to seeing persons under great conviction, I must confess that his appearance gave me a tremendous shock. He was writhing in agony, grinding his teeth, and literally gnawing his tongue for pain. He cried out to me, 'Oh, Mr. Finney! I am lost! I am a lost soul!' I was greatly shocked and exclaimed, 'If this be conviction, what is hell?' " [32] Then in proportion to the intensity of the misery endured come the glory and rapture of the spiritual deliverance. In the words of Finney as to himself: "I wept aloud with joy and love; and I do not know but I should say, I literally bellowed out the unutterable gushings of my heart. These waves came over me, and over me, and over me, one after the other until I recollect I cried out, 'I shall die if these waves continue to pass over me.' " [33]   One marked feature of the experience seems to be a complete transformation of the outer world, which is transfigured, glorified, as if seen with new and heavenly eyes. The poor plumber in Harold Begbie's "Twice-Born Men" comes out into the streets alone: "He was glad in himself, and the outside world seemed glad. The pavements shone with fire, the distance was a haze of bright light, the leaves of all the trees in the road, he says, seemed like hands waving to him. He felt that he had come out of a nightmare into a dream." [34]

The great question, of course, as to such spiritual changes is that of their endurance, especially when they involve entire revolutions of moral conduct. The debate on this point will probably never cease. No doubt there are innumerable cases of backsliding more or less complete. But it is also certain that the alteration is in many cases permanent. As Professor Underwood says, "The most remarkable fruit of conversion is seen in the manner in which it has brought about complete and permanent deliverance from every known sin." [35]

THE GROWTH OF A SOUL

The temptation to refer to some of the endless celebrated instances of conversion is difficult to resist. Probably that of Saint Paul at the very foundation of Christianity is the most famous. One cannot overlook Saint Augustine's passionately dramatic account of the struggle in his soul between the two fiercely contending wills, first one prevailing and then the other, until the note of childish song, "Tolle! Lege!" "Tolle! Lege!" bade him turn to his Bible and find relief. Or a very different type is Jonathan Edward's story of the little girl of four years old who went through the spiritual agonies and experienced the spiritual ecstasy.[36]

What comes home to one most is what comes nearest to oneself. If one cannot record one's own conversion, it is at least intensely startling to have a person whom one loves most dearly, whom one considers to have the clearest intelligence and the sanest, wisest, most reasonable outlook upon life use such words as follow: "I can't stop now to write a long letter, but I must just write a word to tell you that I have found the Lord or the Lord has found me in a way I have never dreamed of—that the blessing of his presence which I have longed for and prayed for has become mine as a permanent possession. I have had it before at times in a fitful way, but I have been an unprofitable, halting follower, my usefulness hindered by miserable doubts and uncertainties. God has taken them away and with Him to work in me to do the uncertain, impossible things, I enter a new life of service. I am so intensely ashamed of the past, but that is forgiven me. I am glorying in the joy of the present and future. . . . You know I have always felt that the Lord has a great work for you and you yourself have said that you would be a preacher if you only had a message. You are going to have one. **I know it.**" Alas, the message never came.

It is interesting to get Moody's ideas as to the general matter of conversion, as they are scattered through his sermons, though the ideas may not be very profound or very consistent. He admits that conversion may be at times a gradual process, and he constantly urges that its value and especially its external sign must consist in permanent and radical alteration of life. At the same time, as was natural with his methods and with his activities, he stresses most of all the sudden elements, the miraculous transformation by which the spirit of God enters into a soul and makes it over. "Seventeen years afterward, I was born from above; I got life from God; a new life, distinct and separate from the natural life. I got a life that is as everlasting as God's life; a life that there is no end to: eternal life. How did I get it? By receiving the Word of God into my heart." [37] Again: "Salvation is instantaneous. I admit that a man may be converted so that he cannot tell when he crossed the line between death and life, but I also believe a man may be a thief one moment and a saint the next. I believe a man may be as vile as hell itself one moment, and be saved the next." [38]

As to Moody's own personal experience we have abundant record both from others and from himself. The external facts are simple. When he first went to Boston as a boy of seventeen, he had lived with religion, but he had not felt it. He went to Dr. Kirk's Mount Vernon Street Congregational Church and slept through sermons which he did not understand. A benevolent member got him into the Sunday School, but his ignorance was alarming. Even when he was ready to join the church, the committee at first thought him so ill qualified that for some time they refused him admission, and when they at last yielded, it was with a foreboding that he would do them more injury than credit. They certainly had no perception of the astounding future.

The internal process is more curious still. There seems to have been comparatively little in Moody's case of the previous struggle and anguish. He was not particularly conscious of sin or particularly overwhelmed with remorse. When it seemed appropriate and suitable to be converted, he was converted. Even his description of the resultant ecstasy sounds to me a little like something he had heard of: "I thought the old sun shone a good deal brighter than it ever had before. . . . I fell in love with the birds. I had never cared for them before." [39] He seems never to have felt an oppressive need of salvation as he never certainly entertained a doubt of possessing it. On the other hand, after the conversion there were periods of apparently much greater struggle: "There was another time when God was calling me into higher service, to go out and preach the gospel all over the land, instead of staying in Chicago. I fought against it for months; but the best thing I ever did was when I surrendered my will, and let the will of God be done in me." [40] And after such struggle the acceptance and submission were accompanied by proportionate

48

ecstasy. As he told Dr. Torrey, "The power of God fell upon him as he walked up the street and he had to hurry off to the house of a friend and ask that he might have a room by himself, and in that room he stayed alone for hours; and the Holy Ghost came upon him filling his soul with such joy that at last he had to ask God to withhold His Hand, lest he die on the spot from very joy." [41]

It cannot be questioned, however, that with Moody the essence of conversion was the impulse to convert others. His own account of this is irresistible in its vividness: "I remember when I was first converted here in Boston and I used to hear Dr. Kirk's sermons—after I was converted I did hear them; I didn't hear them before, I was sound asleep. But when God waked me up and I did hear them, it seemed as if God set me afire. I could not sit still, but I had to go out to preach." [42] Not for him was the passive joy of dreaming of heaven and divine perfection. He was a worker and to him religion meant work. Selling shoes was very well; but buying souls was infinitely better. He had been waked up by having the secret of the universe sounded in his ears. He was going forth to proclaim it to millions of sinners so that they might never sleep in their damning lethargy again. Though he was unlike Shelley in every other respect, he was at least like him in that he had a passion for reforming the world.

VII

Boston was hardly the most favorable field for such fiery, spontaneous, somewhat unchastened energies as animated the new convert. Chicago offered a more encouraging atmosphere, and he went there in 1856. At first he continued to sell shoes. But with time religious interests became so engrossing that he abandoned the direct effort for livelihood, and even after he was married, he trusted to God altogether for support. The struggle involved in giving up business was severe. He had been successful, and his earlier ambition had been to make money, not perhaps so much for the money as for the satisfaction of achievement. "The height of my ambition had been to be a successful merchant, and if I had known that meeting was going to take that ambition out of me, I might not have gone." [43] But he was getting glimpses of a far bigger achievement, of a more satisfying success, and more and more he gave himself up to what he considered to be the will of God. He said to Dr. Torrey, "Torrey, if I believed that God

MOODY'S BODY GUARD.

The crude material from which he evolved his first Sunday-school class in Chicago.

WILL IT PAY?

MOODY'S BODY GUARD.

D. L. Moody's first Sunday-school class in Chicago.

IT DOES PAY.

wanted me to jump out of that window, I would jump." [44] You cannot doubt that he would have done it.

But as a religious teacher he had everything to learn. He did not look it, to begin with. His heavy, solid, stolid face and figure, though capable of sudden illumination, did not generally suggest spiritual comfort. His extreme ignorance hampered him at every step. His first, last, and only weapon of warfare was the English Bible; yet he could not read the Bible in those early days without stumbling woefully over the hard words.

Preaching of course he knew nothing of, and indeed at the start the idea of becoming a preacher would have seemed ludicrous to even his high-soaring spirit. In the church which he joined on going to Chicago he was rejected as a Sunday-School teacher. But he went out into the highways and got together a class of young reprobates whom no one else could handle. The spirit in which he did it shows in his later comment: "There is no place in the world that is so fascinating as a live Bible class." [45] And again there is his own description of how he went to work: "I was two years trying to find what my work was before I succeeded. When I commenced to speak in meetings the grown people would [not?] hear me. I could notice them squirm their shoulders when I got up. But at last I went out one Sunday and got hold of eighteen ragged boys. That was about the happiest Sunday I ever experienced. If I couldn't teach others I could take them where there were those who could." [46] Preaching came upon him, as it were by accident. He went to a Sunday-School convention with a friend. The other expected speakers gave out or failed. The friend spoke while Moody prayed for him. Then the friend took the praying and Moody took the speaking turn. "He poured out such a torrent of red-hot words—words so full of spiritual life and vigor—that the people stared in surprise, and then were moved profoundly by the eloquence of this unlettered, rugged young giant from Chicago." [47] Sixty conversions ensued on the spot. The gift of tongues was born with him: all that was needed was practice and opportunity.

Also, back of the tongue was the torrent rush of incomparable energy, the unfailing muscular and nervous strength, which make him stand out even among revivalists, who are not a particularly spineless generation. Whatever there was to be done, he did it, not only his own work, but the work of others, and found out things to do which others never imagined. He seemed tireless. No difficulty, no opposition, could daunt him, and no fatigue could wear him out. When he had established his irregular church, he had to cover a vast parish, a parish in which pastoral calls meant more than anywhere else. He would dart from house to house, burst in, and cry: "You know me. I am Moody. This is Deacon De Golyer, this is Deacon Thane, this is Brother Hitchcock. Are you all well? Do you all come to church and Sunday-School? Have you all the coal you need for the winter? Let us pray." [48] And they prayed, decorously, but expeditiously, and he hurried on to the next, and the number he would deal with in one afternoon left his attendants gasping.

Even in the early days his extraordinary talent for business management began to show itself and perhaps needed cultivation less than some others. He knew how to lead men, all kinds of men, to make them do what he wanted, to make them work, to make them want to work, which is the hardest of all. Others found the money problem difficult. It was easy to him. In the first place he convinced men of his absolute honesty, and then he made them give. But he not only got money, he knew how to use it, and he used not only money, but every other means to make his enterprises successful. Other ministers preached to empty pews. Not he, he wouldn't, and didn't. "It was pretty hard to preach to empty chairs. But I got a few interested in the meeting and then we got out some hand-bills that cost about sixty cents a thousand, and then we took some of the young men and got them to come together every night in the hall, and we gave them some tea and they prayed together; and they took these hand-bills and went out on the street, and every man had a district, and they visited every saloon and billiard hall and bowling alley, and there was not a man who came within a mile of the building but got from one to half a dozen of these invitations to come to that meeting. And when a man was converted we yoked him up with another, two and two, and sent them out to bring others, and that is the way we did it, and we have always had an audience ever since." [49] And if any man knew a better way, he was welcome to come and try it. Thus this irregular pastor built up a prosperous and efficient church, a church that was thoroughly alive, and his fellow preachers became extremely curious to know how he did it.

THE GROWTH OF A SOUL

Best of all, this early Chicago experience of ten years or more was an inestimable apprenticeship in the art of handling souls. Dr. Goss draws a vivid picture of Moody's contact during these years with all sorts of people and the advantage he derived from it for his future work.[50] No society was too low or too rough for him to plunge into with flawless courage and considerate tact. No group of men of the world was too wealthy or too hardened for him to venture upon with absolute dignity and with a keen sense of the side of his undertaking, whatever it was, that would appeal to them. He might fail, but it did not disturb him in the least. All he had to do was to turn somewhere else and begin again. In these human dealings his Civil War experience was of the greatest value to him. He had seen men suffer and struggle and die, and he knew what it meant. In all circumstances, no matter what were the surroundings or the conditions, he went right at the heart, and knew how to find it. In working with men and for them he learned to know them, and instinctively, unconsciously, his own nature was broadened and made more human, or rather, the vast humanity which was born in him and was the secret of his power was released and trained and deepened by his contact with all these lives, rich and poor, gentle and simple, honest and dishonest, who all wanted something which he was able to give them, largely because of his immense confidence that he had it to give. He went up and down the world, asking all he met, "Are you a Christian? Are you a Christian?" And the reason why he was listened to and not struck in the face was no doubt partly because he was not very strikable, but also what is indicated in the remark of one of those whom he labored to convert, though not with perfect success: "Mr. Moody, I thank you. I have been prayed *for,* and prayed *at,* a great many times; but no one ever prayed *with* me until now." [51]

Thus equipped and partly trained, but still and always learning his business, the call came to Moody to leave Chicago, and wander over the wide world, an evangelist, a bringer of good tidings, a messenger of joy. He sailed for England, in 1873, with Sankey, who was already loyally supporting him by passionate song, to begin their triumphant tour of the British Isles. At this point we shall gain most by leaving the chronological order and making a more thorough dissection of the various elements of the evangelist's purpose, career, achievement, and character.

CHAPTER II

I

WE should establish first what Moody started with and what he had behind him, and let us begin with the matter of doctrine. Pascal, of whom Moody assuredly knew nothing, said, "I do not think it worth while to probe the speculations of Copernicus, but we should simply remember this, that all life centers upon the question whether the soul is mortal or immortal." [1] To answer this question of Pascal, Moody used nothing, asked for nothing, wanted nothing but the English Bible. His reliance upon this authority was complete and unlimited. The grotesqueness of founding a religion upon a translation, when no translation ever conveys the original, did not affect him in the slightest. His mother had read to him the English Bible. He had sucked salvation from it. That was enough. Again, that the Bible was a historical growth, that in its earlier portion it represented the struggle of a petty oriental people to record the confused incoherence of its passionate spiritual development, meant nothing to him. It was the word of God, whole and entire. To question it was infidelity and led to hell. The contradictions and inconsistencies did not trouble him. Either they were explicable, that is, he could explain them, to his own satisfaction, or it was the divine will that we should let them alone. And he has this delightful final word on all such difficulties: "The Bible was not made to understand." [2] His entire and perfect adherence to this irrefragable authority is summed up in the beginning of the little book on Heaven: "We believe that the Bible is inspired because there is nothing in it that could *not* have come from God. . . . There is nothing in the Bible that is not wise, and there is nothing in it that is not good." [3]

To such a mental attitude the most literal acceptance of all the Bible narratives and statements was possible and easy. One of Moody's most ardent admirers speaks of "the extraordinary voracity of his faith." [4] Matthew Arnold, commenting on some of the more surprising Biblical incidents, says that even the most extreme literalist admits that these are figurative but those who know more than he find much else that is figurative also. There is little sign that Moody inclined to the figurative ever, though no doubt even he had his moments. The story of the Flood and the Ark was as historical to him as the record of the Civil War. As for the adventure of Jonah, which is usually regarded as a test stumbling-block, he simply riots in it. Christ believed the story of Jonah and likened his resurrection to it. After that, what is to be said? To be sure, it is argued that a whale's mouth is somewhat limited for such substantial deglutition. What of that? "The book of Jonah says that *God prepared a great fish to swallow* Jonah. Couldn't God make a fish large enough to swallow Jonah? If God could create a world, I think He could create a fish large enough to swallow a *million* men." [5] Then, after these extravagances, he will hit upon one of those simple, searching words that go right to the heart, as when he quotes the reply of a young convert who was asked, "How can you prove that the Bible is inspired?" and answered, "Because it inspires me." [6]

It is obvious that one who approached the Bible in this literal fashion could have had little interest in modern critical scholarship, in the attempt to read the Christian mysteries in the light of nineteenth century science and philosophy. To Moody all such investigation was misleading and dangerous and emanated directly from the devil. To be sure, as we have seen, he was a most assiduous student. He had oceans of commentaries and toiled over them with the slow and weary diligence of an unaccustomed brain, but his purpose was to extract moral and spiritual nourishment for the millions whom he was called upon to feed. We know that he limited his choice of books to such as could help him to understand *the* book; but he did not appreciate that really to understand the Bible one must read not only pious commentaries, not only the meditations of theologians, but that strange, bewildering Shakespeare, and even the novels which Moody detested but which record the widest wanderings and the wildest passions of the human heart. When men talked to him about the higher criticism, about subtle interpretations and figurative language, he cried impatiently, "That's just the way men talk now and just figure away everything." [7] To him it was the Bible, the whole Bible, and nothing but the Bible. He speaks with infinite scorn of the minister who, being afflicted with doubts, finally decided to cut out of the sacred book everything that could be open to question, and in the end there was nothing left but the cover. Dr. Goss tells pathetically of his feeling that in the later years the great preacher did not gain so many converts, and Goss recounts his own effort to explain to him that it was because he did not use other methods for other times. "He fixed those great deep eyes upon me with one of those long stares which seemed to penetrate into my very soul, and shook his head. What I said did not appeal to him. He knew no other methods." [8] How I should like to have Moody's version of that interview.

Of course Moody professed not to deal much in doctrine anyway. His idea was that he stuck to the fundamentals and left the theoretical embroidery to the theologians to fuss over. When a lady came to him and said, "I want to be frank with you, I want you to know that I do not believe in your theology," he answered. "My theology! I didn't know I had any. I wish you would tell me what my theology is." [9] Yet this man was constantly pouring out theological propositions with an abundance which is simply staggering to the unenlightened mind. "A good many live on negations. They are always telling what they *don't* believe. I want a man to tell me what he does believe, not what he does not believe. And I like to meet a positive man." [10] All he had to do was to look in the glass.

The fact is that he thought he was dealing with self-evident truths, he thought he was based upon axioms so fundamental that they could not be classed at all with the divagations of theology. In reality, though he had not read the theologians widely, he had listened for years to sermons from Doctor Kirk and others founded on recondite metaphysical reasoning and his whole system had become saturated with a cloudy mass of doctrine which was made over and fused and vivified in the fire of his passionate heart and speech. What he believed may perhaps be not unfairly summed up something as follows: that the Bible was absolutely the word of God, that the Bible taught that man was originally sinful and had fallen from grace, that the Son of God had sacrificed himself to atone for our sins, and that by accepting the atonement of his blood and showing that acceptance in our lives we may escape hell and be assured of heaven. If this is simple, it is difficult to imagine what is complicated, and such a mass of implicit theology certainly forms a tough morsel for one who finds it hard to accept a single sentence of the Apostles' Creed. Yet to Moody it was essential and there was no salvation without it.

In other words, an obscure, elaborate reasoning process worked in his close, compact, ardent intellect to violently logical, or illogical conclusions. Like many others who have not reflected upon the nature of reason, he did not appreciate that, while it is all we have for theoretical investigation or for practical action, when the far surer guidance of instinct fails us, it is yet a most delicate and fragile instrument, liable to be jarred and perverted by every flaw and tremor of passion, and quite capable, under the influence of desire and prejudice, of working to exactly opposite ends. To be sure, he sometimes belabors reason with his furious vigor. He is even said to have declared that "the Voice of Reason is the voice of hell." [11] Just as, on the other side, he could declaim with equal energy against feeling: "Feeling! Feeling! Feeling! I wish that word was banished from the inquiry room. If that word is touched in the word of God, I haven't been able to find it. . . . I thank God I have a better foundation for my faith than feeling." [12] That is, he placed his reliance upon faith itself. He did not know that to some persons faith is simply reason gone to seed, and that to others more sympathetic, but perhaps un-regenerate, faith is a more or less unconscious reasoning process associated with the transfiguring glory of religious emotion. If he had known, he would not have cared.

Again, as noted in the previous chapter, we have the ignorance of ignorance developing into an assured arrogance of dogmatic positiveness. Moody's admirers constantly proclaim that he was broad and tolerant. On matters that he considered inessential he was charitable to an extraordinary degree. But when it came to the fundamentals, he was iron. He was perhaps the original Fundamentalist, and it is easy to divine what would have been his attitude towards evolution in the controversies that have been recently carried on, though I am not aware that he alludes to the subject more than once: "It is a great deal easier to believe that man was made after the image of God than to believe, as some young men and women are being taught now, that he is the offspring of a monkey." [13] Parenthetically, it is hard to think that, from his point of view, he was not right, and that there is not an eternal conflict, at any rate in the popular mind, between the scientific theory of evolution and the type of Christianity, which to some of us still appears the most efficient type. As Edmond Scherer said, the world will recognize a great gap between thought before Darwin and thought after him. Only perhaps it would be fairer to carry the sin still further back to Copernicus, who demolished man's central position in the universe and left an insignificant mite crawling on a grain of sand, whirled indifferently in the vast processes of cosmic infinitude.

But as to the matter of tolerance, it is extremely curious to watch the interlocking of the two extremes in Moody's doctrine and temperament. His large good-nature and essential kindliness made him friendly and sympathetic with everybody. Probably no Protestant preacher has ever been on better terms with the Catholics and been more commended by them. He himself cried: "If I thought I had one drop of sectarian blood in my veins, I would let it out before I went to bed; if I had one sectarian hair in my head, I would pull it out." [14] Yet, he proclaimed with fervor, "I had rather be narrow and right than broad and wrong;" [15] and he had deeply rooted in his soul the cardinal principle of all intolerance, that belief is voluntary and therefore that unbelief is a sin. He shrieks it from the housetops: "A great many people think that unbelief is a sort of misfortune, but do not know, if you will allow me the expression, it is the damning sin of the world today; that is what unbelief is, the mother of all sin." [16] From such a mental attitude there is but one step to the bonfire methods of Calvin and The Inquisition.

The profound, dissolving character of real intellectual tolerance, based on the humility of utter ignorance, was quite unknown to Moody. The subtle confession of Anatole France, "I love tolerance so much that to me it is dearer than the dearest of beliefs"; the final analysis of Scherer, "The fundamental dogma of intolerance is that there are dogmas, that of tolerance, that there are only opinions," would have been a horror of horrors to Moody: he knew. And there is this to be said for him: pure Truth as a mistress is elusive and deceiving; she lures us up and down the world with the perpetual promise of attainment, but she never fulfills the promise, and at last leaves us unsatisfied, departing with a mocking finger laid upon her lip. Moody's salvation, if you can get it, and millions have, brings with it an enduring peace.

HEAVEN AND HELL

II

So much for Moody's background on the doctrinal side. Now to turn to the side of emotion. The religious revival obviously did not originate with him. On the contrary, it is as old as religion itself, and it is extremely curious to trace Moody's relation to his predecessors.

Professor Underwood's comment upon the Eleusinian Mysteries of Greece is remarkably significant for all revival movements since. The aim of those Mysteries, he says, "was not so much to communicate esoteric doctrine as to create an overpowering impression by the stimulus of collective excitement." [17] I don't know how you could describe more effectively the various revival movements of the early Church, of Catholic enthusiasts, and of brilliant, gifted preachers, like Whitefield and the Wesleys in England and the series, from Jonathan Edwards down, which shook America in the eighteenth and nineteenth centuries, probably by no means ending with Billy Sunday, or the English correlative, the Salvation Army. An acute observer interestingly connects the Protestant and Catholic Churches in this respect, taking conversion as the prime object of revival activity: "The prominence of 'conversion' in practical theology began with the Order of the Jesuits and was borrowed from them by the Pietists and Methodists of last century." [18] But the general emotional stimulus is certainly not confined to any sect or to any age.

The eighteenth and early nineteenth century revivals in America seem in some ways to have the most distinctive and specific characteristics, perhaps because they shone out in the comparative monotony of the social life about them. The working and development of these movements have been carefully studied, both by contemporary observers and by more scientific investigators of later days. It appears that in some cases the agitation began spontaneously, affecting a few individuals, and then spreading till whole neighborhoods were carried away. In other instances, perhaps in the majority, the revival was a matter of careful planning. A minister, usually inspired by intense zeal for the salvation of multitudes who were dancing upon the borders of hell, but occasionally seeking notoriety for himself, would gradually arouse excitement and enthusiasm. Or a wandering evangelist would go from town to town, carrying with him the torch of spiritual disturbance and applying it wherever it seemed to be most needed and most likely to do good. Favorable agents were seized upon in the community itself and made the instruments of conveying the glad tidings to others. In one of the earlier revivals, for example, a girl of fourteen "was carried over the whole township from house to house, instructing, admonishing, and even praying. Indeed, my informant said, much as if he had been speaking of the competition in a race-course, that 'there was not a *man* in the town that could pray with her.' " [19] Perhaps I may conclude this brief sketch of revival movements in general with the somewhat unfriendly comments of so acute a recent analyst as Dr. Joseph Collins: Revivals "rarely last longer than the active period of the chief revivalist's lifetime, ten to twenty years. They have been invariably followed by what may properly be called religious lethargy. Their occurrence constitutes a cycle made up of the revival; the apathy of emotional bluntness that follows it, characterized by the ascendancy of materialistic display; then a period of crass neglect of religion, apparent deafness to the exhortations of its sane, temperate, earnest advocates, and finally, the revival again. In fact, revivals run a course, almost parallel to a disorder that is usually known as maniac depressive insanity." [20]

It is necessary to summarize to a certain extent the more hysterical manifestations connected with early revival activity in order to grasp its full spiritual significance. It should be remembered that not only the average Christian and the average minister, but men of such trained intelligence and profound spiritual discernment as Wesley and Jonathan Edwards regarded these manifestations as the direct result of the working of the Holy Spirit and not as symptoms of pathological infirmity, as would be usually the case to-day. What wonder was it that sensitive, high-strung temperaments, or even temperaments that were more normal, were thrown out of balance by the persistent atmosphere of hell? Hell was not only shouted from the pulpit, it murmured with the crickets in the peaceful chimney-corner, it intruded its baleful suggestion into the routine of the school-room. Of all its innumerable developments I think few affect me more than the image of so sane, thoughtful, and practical a woman as Mary Lyon getting up before her crowd of sensitive, adolescent girls at Mount Holyoke and flinging hell at them until the flames seemed to glare and crackle under their feet.[21] Surely it was natural for Mrs. Stowe to write of these theological agitations, "With many New England women at this particular period, when life was so retired and so cut off from outward sources of excitement, *thinking* grew to be a disease."[22]

In the full fury of the great revival meetings the climax of hysterical outburst was sometimes extraordinary and to the colder reader of to-day merely horrible. Not only women but strong men fell upon the floor and remained for hours insensible. They writhed in agony, and shouted in mortal fear. And the evangelist, when he could get their attention, piled on the distress and disturbance, all with the object of making the final relief more intense and glorious. Finney cries in ecstasy: "If I had had a sword in each hand, I could not have cut them off the seats as fast as they fell." And then when the right moment is reached, he shouts to them: "You are not in hell yet; and now let me direct you to Christ."[23]

In the more primitive western portions of the United States the phenomena in the early nineteenth century were still more remarkable. Sometimes the audience fell to barking like dogs, sometimes they were overtaken with contagious convulsions called "the jerks," when they shook and quivered and brandished their limbs in unconscious reminiscence of the savage antics of their wilder ancestors. And the more extravagant the manifestations were, the more souls were believed to be redeemed from perdition.

It is well to emphasize all this, so as to bring out the fact that it was intolerable and disgusting to Moody and in every instance he discouraged it and absolutely eliminated it from his activity everywhere. Excitement, yes; he wanted excitement and believed in it, but a true, fruitful, spiritual excitement, not the morbid manifestations of encroaching hysteria. No doubt his modified attitude was partly that of his age; but this was not wholly true, since after his time we find the Salvation Army pursuing the old tactics: "Big men, as well as women, fell to the ground, lay there for some time as if dead, overwhelmed with the Power from on High." [24]

In studying all these violent symptoms, in England and still more in America, one cannot help feeling that we have in them the sudden outbreak of the emotional, esthetic nature too long and too harshly repressed, and one is reminded of Matthew Arnold's oft-repeated comment that in its reaction against the excesses of the Renaissance the English spirit entered the prison of Puritanism and had the key turned upon it for two hundred and fifty years. All the grace, all the gayety, "dance and Provençal song and sunburnt mirth," all the social diversions which relieved and expressed that emotional nature in southern Europe, were treated by the Puritans as a device of the devil. When they came over here from Elizabethan England, they brought God with them, but they left Shakespeare behind. And all that Shakespeare represents revenged itself by these fantastic contortions of emotional excess. The excellent and not unsympathetic English observer Dewey asked an American friend why, when his people were so sober and restrained in everything else, they should have these great excitements in religion: "How is it that you who do everything else by *calculation* trust these to passion?" [25] The answer of the American is not recorded, but it would obviously be that the universal repression must force an outlet in the weakest spot.

After which it should not be forgotten that under these more repellent and objectionable symptoms there was not only a generation of spiritual joy but of moral dignity and self-control.

D. L. MOODY: A WORKER IN SOULS

For the finer elements it is pleasant to quote a lovely passage of Jonathan Edwards, because it is so different from the horrors too apt to be associated with him: "The soul of a true Christian . . . appeared like such a little white flower as we see in the spring of the year; low and humble on the ground, opening its bosom to receive the pleasant beams of the sun's glory; rejoicing, as it were, in a calm rapture; diffusing around a sweet fragrancy; standing peacefully and lovingly in the midst of other flowers round about, all in like manner opening their bosoms to drink in the light of the sun." [26] But there was not only a calm ecstasy, there was a soaring aspiration, a sweeping detachment from the meager things of this world, a vast transcendency which reached its almost unbelievable climax in the willingness, even the passionate desire, to be damned for the glory of God; and however extravagant such a willingness may seem to more prosaic states of mind, it must be admitted that it added a certain largeness and splendor to human nature.

Then comes, of course, the question of the permanence of these revival effects. Dr. Collins speaks of the reaction of indifference. It is impossible to deny it wholly. The human spirit cannot long exist on such heights. But statements like the following in relation to the Great Awakening of 1741 are significant, even if one feels them to be somewhat exaggerated: "It cannot be doubted that at least 50,000 souls were added to the churches of New England out of a population of about 250,-000, as it is estimated, . . . a fact sufficient to revolutionize, as indeed it did, the religious and moral character and to determine the destinies, of the country." [27] With regard to later revivals the testimony is of course conflicting according to its source, but the words of the New York *Times* after the Moody revival of 1876 are surely worth consideration: "The drunken have become sober, the vicious virtuous, the worldly and self-seeking unselfish, the impure pure, the youth have started with generous aims, the old have been stirred from grossness. A new hope has lifted up hundreds of human beings, a new consolation has come to the sorrowful; and a better principle has entered the sordid life of the day through the labors of these plain men." [28]

What I should like to know is how much Moody studied the history of the revivalists who preceded him. Obviously he reproduced many of their methods and adopted many of their ideas, while sensibly correcting their mistakes. He is said to have read assiduously the sermons of the Welsh preacher Evans and to have been much affected by them. But I imagine he imbibed the older traditions rather by hearsay than by direct study. He refers occasionally to Wesley, rarely to any of the others. And his own natural genius for the work in hand was sufficient to lead him to results without much training.

Another question which much perplexes me is, What would Christ himself have said if he could have been present at an active revival meeting? I feel myself utterly at a loss to conjecture the answer and I leave the reader to think of it. But in this connection I am glad to quote another beautiful sentence of Jonathan Edwards, showing the noble restraint and humble moderation of the man, in spite of all his intellectual excesses. He is reprehending some undue violence in the manner of the preachers of his day and he says: "The man Christ Jesus when he was upon earth had doubtless as great a sense of the infinite greatness and importance of the eternal things and the worth of souls as any have now; but there is not the least appearance in his history of his taking any such course or manner of exhorting others." [29] Which seems to me worth considering by all revivalists, though Edwards was one himself.

III

Having thus established both the doctrinal and the emotional background against which the burly, energetic figure of Moody stands out, we are in a better position to appreciate what he taught and how he taught it. It must first be understood that there was little or nothing of the mystic in his religious conceptions, any more than in those of the Bible or the Jews.

The effort of the mystic is to achieve, so far as possible, identity with the Divine, to lose this narrow, limited, restless human spirit in the limitless immensity of God. Intellectually it is of course often difficult to distinguish this ineffable aspiration from Pantheism, but the distinction has never been better expressed than in the sentence of Goethe: "To the materialist everything is God; to the mystical Pantheist God is everything." [30] There are all degrees of the mystic's rapture, from the temporary ecstasy compatible with a more definite and limited metaphysical creed to permanent self-abandonment and self-oblivion erected into a final and sufficient dogma. What the beauty and fullness of the rapture is cannot be much better exemplified than in the testimony recorded by Edwards: "The soul remained in a kind of heavenly elysium and did as it were swim in the rays of Christ's love, like a little mote swimming in the beams of the sun that come in at a window. The heart was swallowed up in a kind of glow of Christ's love coming down as a constant stream of sweet light, at the same time that the soul all flowed out in love to him; so that there seemed to be a constant flowing and reflowing from heart to heart. The soul dwelt on high, was lost in God, and seemed almost to leave the body. The mind dwelt in a pure delight that fed and satisfied it; enjoying pleasure without the least sting or any interruption. . . . What was enjoyed in a single minute of the whole space, which was many hours, was worth more than the outward comfort and pleasure of the whole life put together." [31]

It cannot be denied that for the merely external observer the nature of this absorption is difficult to seize. The problem would seem to resolve itself into the eternal struggle between multiplicity and unity. Multiplicity, diversity, endless change, mean weariness, exhaustion, infinite longing for relief and rest, but they also mean life. Unity means escape, tranquillity, repose—but it also means death and nothingness. In the mysticism of the East multiplicity is personified in the ever tantalizing, the elusive, the mocking Maia, and the refuge seems to lie in Nirvana, in entire absorption in the One which is at the bottom of all diversity and is unchangeable for ever and ever. The more passionate Christian mystics play with the same idea, if such deadly earnest can ever be called playing: "When you stop at one thing, you cease to open yourself to the All. For to come to the All you must give up the All. And if you should attain to owning the All, you must own it, desiring Nothing." [32]

Nothing! Somehow the ideal of the mystic, viewed too coldly, approximates Nothing with a fatal logic, and in connection with it one cannot but remember the concluding words of Schopenhauer's great study: "Rather do we freely acknowledge that what remains after the entire abolition of will is for all those who are still full of will certainly nothing; but, conversely, to those in whom the will has turned and has denied itself, this our world, which is so real, with all its suns and milky ways—is nothing." [33]

But these cloudy regions had no charm for D. L.

Moody. His God was astonishingly, or perhaps naturally, like himself, stout, substantial, justice-dispensing, loving and hating, seated on a perfectly concrete throne in a perfectly concrete heaven. Everywhere He is represented with bewilderingly solid humanness. For example, in connection with the parable of the Prodigal Son we are told that God frequently runs when He is in a hurry.[34] In other words, Deity sometimes exchanges the solemn progress of the blackbird for the more frivolous locomotion of the robin. And His habitation is presented as vividly as He Himself. Heaven is above our heads, wherever we are, but we are assured that it is a perfectly tangible and mapable city, like New York, a comparison singularly malodorous, at least to a native of Boston. When we come to a description of its attractions, there is the usual fatal resort to negatives and comparatives. There is no sorrow there, no suffering, no weariness, which dangerously suggests Schopenhauer's nothing, after all. As to its charm, it is better than anything we know, sweeter, lovelier, which is alluring but all rather lamentably indefinite, though why should one expect Moody to succeed where no one else ever has? There is the usual promise of recognition of departed friends; but there is no attempt to resolve the endless problems of perplexity which this always carries with it.

On the other hand, hell is fiercely tangible, and generations of exhorters have had no difficulty whatever in making it so. Some persons tell us that hell has disappeared forever. There was a lady, who had been brought up with a rather austere Calvinism, and who was heard every night to stand over her child's cradle and murmur to him, "Jack, there is no hell, there is no hell, there is no hell." I wonder how she knew. The truth is, so long as self-preservation is the prime motive of human life, and so long as fear is the prime expression of self-preservation, and so long as we have to step from this sun-lit world into an unexplored abyss of darkness, so long will men, openly or secretly, echo the wild anticipations of Claudio,

> "To be worse than worst
> Of those that lawless and incertain thoughts
> Imagine howling,"

and so long will it be possible to speak to them of hell with hideous effect.

As to Moody, it is justly maintained that hell was not the main theme of his teaching. His natural kindness and tenderness made him lean more to love, and the sermons of the English revivalist Moorehouse crystallized this tendency at an early stage in the American's career. Moody proclaimed the gospel of love, that God's mercy was infinite and that no sinner need suffer, if he would repent. At the same time hell was at the bottom of it all and was never forgotten. In one indisputable passage he shouts this aloud, so that no one can overlook it or misunderstand it: "If there is no hell, let us burn our Bibles. Why spend so much time studying the Bible? . . . If I believed there was no hell, you would not find me going from town to town, spending day and night preaching and proclaiming the Gospel and urging men to escape the damnation of hell. I would take things easy." [35] Even so he did not usually dilate on the physical horrors of the nether world, however much he may have believed in them. Doctor Abbott writes: "I think the most terrifying sermon on future punishment I ever heard was one on 'Son, remember.' But it was wholly psychological, a vivid portrayal of what was here and what would be hereafter the anguish of a soul who, looking back, could remember only a life of wasted opportunities, sensual excesses, selfish cruelties." [36]

And if hell was comparatively cloudy, or at

least remote, there was sin, right here in this world, transgression of the commands of God, unescapable except by the road that Moody could point out. And it must be admitted that the constant preoccupation with sin and hell made religion largely negative. The very word that is the keynote of the whole of it, salvation, is negative and nothing else. Even so exquisite a mystic as Saint Teresa can say of heaven that its principal happiness "appears to me to consist in a disregard of all earthly things, and in a peace and glory that dwell in a soul *which rejoices in the bliss of its companions.*" [37] Surely a somewhat pale and colorless conclusion. It is indeed the furious and passionate solicitude for companions in misery, for others, which disguises the negation in Moody's effort. He was enormously, forgetfully busy in positive labor—to save others. But when they were saved, what then? And one is reminded of the pestilent curiosity of the little child who was told that living for others was the only life: "But, mamma, if we are all to live for others, who are the others?"

Evidently, to the charge that his effort was negative Moody would have replied at once that the first duty was to get rid of this strangling burden of hell and sin and that then the mere joy of living would be quite enough for this world or for another. But to one who has given a little more time to profitless reflection it appears that the joy of this world is to a large extent directly or indirectly bound up with what Moody considered sin. If we put aside the grosser pleasures, still the simpler amusements, which he often condemned, the finer raptures of art, the splendor of great tragedy, the high-wrought excitement of romance, which he so ardently rejected, even the subtler charms of color and tone trace something of their attraction to being intertwined with human grief and struggle in a way that makes them queer stuff to construct heaven of. After considering these matters through a long life, some of us are inclined to echo the murmur of Obermann about "this inconceivable universe which contains everything yet does not contain the satisfaction of my desires," [38] to extend the cry of Romeo,

"And shake the yoke of inauspicious stars
From this world-wearied flesh,"

beyond flesh to still more wearied spirit, and to sum up heaven wholly in the longing for complete, untroubled, everlasting peace. But to Moody peace was unknown and unnecessary. Mr. Duffus

Mr. Moody at 25: City Missionary in Chicago.

MR. AND MRS. D. L. MOODY IN 1864 AND IN 1869.

has justly pointed out how unsavory his own heaven would have been to him. Instead, he had little time to think of it, being too preoccupied with the colossal task of saving this world to have much concern to waste upon another.

IV

For to get rid of sin, even to diminish its insolent and pervading empire, would seem to be task enough to preoccupy any one. It is perhaps true that even sin may be exaggerated. There are people in the world, plenty of them, who like to make themselves out to be great and distinguished as sinners, since they cannot as anything else. Moody's own outcry suggests something abnormal: "For my own part, I would a thousand times sooner have the leprosy of the body eating my eyes out, and my feet and arms, I would rather be loathsome in the sight of my fellow-men than die with the leprosy of sin in my soul, and be damned." [39] So does the confession of Edwards: "When others have expressed the sense they have had of their own wickedness by saying that it seemed to them they were as bad as the devil himself, I thought their expression seemed faint and feeble to represent my wickedness." [40] So again

85

does Pascal: "The true and only virtue is hate of oneself." [41] The obsession of sin in introspective and neurotic persons is no doubt thoroughly abnormal and unhealthy; yet there have been millions of such persons and they suffer.

Again, it is certain that in the last half century, under the subtle influence of evolutionary teaching, the moral emphasis has shifted to an extraordinary extent. In the minds of vast numbers who are not directly conscious of the change morality has altered to expediency and an old-fashioned sin has simply become a new-fashioned mistake. All the same, the moral consciousness is grounded pretty deeply in the human spirit. No one will accuse Lord Morley of being unduly pietistic; yet Lord Morley wrote, in connection with Emerson: He "has little to say of that horrid burden and impediment on the soul which the churches call sin and which, by whatever name we call it, is a very real catastrophe in the moral nature of man." [42] There are few men and women who have not battled with temptation in some form or other, who have not known enough of that mad struggle, of its devilish insinuations, its subtle and ever shifting arguments, its perpetual recurrence when you think it has been crushed forever, to feel the benefit of anything that will assuage or banish it. There are many, many who in the bitterest moments of that struggle have found that prayer, whether its agency be merely subjective or objectively divine, comes like the dew of heaven to comfort and relieve. And when the struggle has ended in defeat, many of those who took most pride in having disposed of primitive morality find themselves tormented by agonies of regret and remorse which are just as keen by whatever scientific name you call them. The last volume of the Diary of Samuel Pepys gives a sufficiently poignant record of such agonies in one who was neither morbid nor neurotic, but a hardened, practical man of the world.

It might easily be felt, then, that to save souls from sin was the noblest of all human efforts. To be sure, one result of such a preoccupation was that sinners grew to be one's main interest. It was often charged against Moody that he cared nothing for good people and did not wish to associate with them, that his preference was for drunkards, blacklegs, and harlots, and that the spice of their reformation was what made life interesting. The charge, though absurdly exaggerated in regard to Moody as compared with some other evangelists, is true enough to have a certain significance. To a temperament like Moody's work was all of life and his work did not lie among the good who did not need him. The strange cry of General Booth, "I hungered for hell," [43] might have been echoed by Moody, though I do not know that it was. The good were no pasture for him. And he would never have been imposed upon, as was Emerson's Friar Bernard, who set out to convert the world and found to his surprise that the world did not need converting so very badly, after all. In fact, with Moody the good get little grace and short shrift. Moral, yes, charitable, yes, kindly, yes; but how far do these things go in a world where there is none good but God? "I have often heard good people say that our meetings were doing good, they were reaching the drunkards, and gamblers, and harlots; but they never realized that they needed the grace of God for themselves." [44]

For Moody's fundamental quarrel with the good was that they thought themselves so, whereas there was little to choose in reality between them and the drunkards and the harlots, oftentimes only the insignificant difference of a temptation or an opportunity. He would have utterly resented the naïve remark of Joseph de Maistre, "I know nothing about the conscience of a rascal, but I do know that of an honest man: it is something frightful." Moody would have queried, why an honest man? It is in the highest degree curious to trace the intertwining of works and faith in his energetic common sense. He always took a practical view of life and in such a view the importance of good works could not be overestimated. He emphasizes it again and again, and with reiterated insistence he takes good works, a better, purer, higher life, as the only substantial and satisfactory sign of the transformation that has been wrought within.

At the same time, for the individual soul good works are nothing, simply nothing, compared with the essential salvation which can never come from good works at all. "We are a bad lot, the whole of us, by nature. It is astonishing how the devil does blind us and makes us think we are so naturally good. . . . The first man born of woman was a murderer. Sin leaped into the world full grown, and the whole race has been bad all the way down. Man is naturally bad." [45] Duty, mere duty, the slow, laborious, hopeless effort to perfect self by the painful exercise of fragile human will, he cannot speak of it with contempt enough. The only refuge, the only escape, the only hope is through faith in the redeeming Christ, the only means of coming to him is through passionate, humble, self-forgetful, contrite prayer. And one wonders whether prayer to-day is really the effective, pervading agency that it was even in Moody's day. There is formal prayer enough in the churches. One is sure that an anguished, torn, broken heart instinctively turns to prayer as it always did. But has not the same subtle, insinuating acceptance of the cold laws of scientific necessity which has weakened the sense of sin, tarnished the splendor of prayer also? How many persons to-day can even understand the meaning of the impressive account of universal prayer in a time of revival given by Finney? "Indeed, the town was full of prayer. Go where you would, you heard the voice of prayer. Pass along the street, and if two or three Christians happened to be together, they were praying. Wherever they met, they prayed." [46]

To Moody at any rate prayer was the road, always open, and leading to the direct personal acceptance of the atoning sacrifice of Christ. And the development of this talisman of Christ's sacrifice, and the overwhelming belief in it, are at once the most astonishing and the most natural thing in the world: astonishing in that any one should suppose that what may seem to the outsider a mere verbal hocus-pocus should have power to remove in a moment the great burden of life; natural in that the burden is so crushing, so destructive, and by ordinary means so utterly irremovable, that the desperate soul turns with a gasp of relief to a refuge so sure, so simple, and apparently so efficacious.

To Moody it was absolutely efficacious. He never had one tremor of doubt about the efficacity. "God so loved the world that he gave His only begotten Son, that whosoever believeth in him should not perish but have life everlasting." That was the sum of religion. And Moody loved above all to figure the sacrifice of Christ in the mystical symbol of his blood. He preached on the Blood of Christ, he constantly referred to it, it was by that cleansing power that the world must be purified and made whole, and might be rid forever of its sin: "Not *some* of them; He takes them *all* away. You may pile up your sins till they rise like a dark mountain, and then multiply them by ten thousand for those you cannot think of; and after you have tried to enumerate all the sins you have ever committed, just let me bring one verse in, and that mountain will melt away: 'The blood of Jesus Christ, His Son, cleanseth us from ALL sin.' " [47] To some of us, at any rate, whether we can accept this doctrine or not, it seems that the enormous, unparalleled growth and power and majesty of Christianity in the last nineteen hundred years depend upon it.

V

And further it must be emphasized and repeated that salvation is needed not only for actual sin, but that the good, if there are such, require it just as well as sinners. And here I want to protest against the tone of patronage so often used in regard to the work of Moody, the tone which angered him so much, the assumption that his teaching might do well enough for the ignorant and vile, but that the cultured few could get along without it. I suppose that the suggestion of such a tone will creep into these pages, but the writer of them disclaims it utterly. If there appears to be an attitude of aloofness, it springs not from a doubt of the value of what is to be got, but from a sense of the difficulty of getting it.

There is salvation from the objective misery of life, the pain, the grief, the anguish, the disappointment, and at best the blighting weariness, which we all hide and fight against, but cannot escape. Saint Paul emphasized this, not to speak of Homer and Job before him. The great pessimists have stated it often enough. Take the simple definition of Goncourt: "Life is a nightmare between two nothings." Take the ampler splendor of Leopardi's arraignment, which may be denied and disputed, but can hardly be disposed of completely. Take the desolate outcry of Madame Du Deffand, which states the pessimist position all the more forcibly from making no pretense to philosophical thoroughness: "For my part, I confess that I have but one fixed idea, one feeling, one sorrow, one misfortune, the regret for having been born: there is no rôle that could be played upon the world's wide stage to which I should not prefer annihilation; yet, what will seem to you utterly illogical, even if I had the most assured evidence of a return to nothingness, I should none the less live in horror of death. . . . Teach me how to endure life or to face the end of it without repugnance." [48]

It will be said that these bitter complainers all led unhappy lives, through fault or misfortune. Very well, let us hear Goethe, who is universally regarded as having been one of the most happy, fortunate, and successful of men. This is Goethe's testimony, after a long life: "I will say nothing against the course of my existence. But at bottom it has been nothing but pain and burden, and I can affirm that during the whole of my seventy-five years I have not had four weeks of genuine well being. It is but the perpetual rolling of a rock that must be raised up again forever." [49]

And as this is for the external misery of life, the accidents which circumstance inflicts upon us, so there is the internal torment, the anguish of doubt and question and perpetual, reiterated, vain attempt to solve or put aside the mystery of things, a torment none the less real because it often seems willful and within our control if we would. No doubt a great part of this misery is caused by religion as well as cured by it. One thinks of the suffering endured by Cowper through a long life, by Cowper and by millions of others, until one is almost driven to the petulant outcry that a Deity who could not only bear that his creatures should suffer as humanity does but could allow his own agents of salvation to make it suffer must be himself the incarnation and embodiment of hell. And one remembers the bitter comment of the French cynic that the best compliment one can pay to God is not to believe in him. "I never found an infidel satisfied; they want Christ to satisfy them," says Moody himself.[50] It is at any rate certain that those who have thought till they analyzed away sin and hell and reduced God himself to the shadow of a shade do not find their life of question a life of bliss. There is Sainte-Beuve who proclaimed to the end that his work was only a soothing drug to get rid of the infinite burden of the dragging, poignant, intolerable hours. And we read in the recent confessions of Anatole France, who had had a life as apparently fortunate and triumphant as Goethe's and who had analyzed that life and all others to the dregs: "In all the world the unhappiest creature is man."[51]

It is interesting and tragic to think of the innumerable varied forms of escape that men have sought from this universal despair. More than two thousand years ago there was the Roman poet Lucretius, who had very much the ardent missionary spirit of a Moody. If men would listen to him, all these evils, at least the imaginary ones, might be cleared away. It was religion, with its cruel teachings, its doctrine of a life of torment after death, that caused the worst of human woes. And

D. L. MOODY: A WORKER IN SOULS

Lucretius's remedy, flung at mankind with the tender fury of a Moody, was simply eternal and complete annihilation. Or there is Emerson, with his remote, serene, Concord optimism. The world is good, it must be good, of course, since God is. Shut your eyes to the evil. Live with the good and the good will live with you. Alas, how many of us can accomplish neither. Or again, I hear the gentle, mocking song of our Shakespearean clown, making no pretensions to philosophy, or to wide-mouthed preaching, dissolving the misery of the moment in the all-understanding smile of the eternal. But, alas, again, this attitude is impossible for too many of us.

And then comes along this commercial dealer in the subtle wares of the spirit, D. L. Moody, cries out, "Are you a Christian?," and offers us the greatest of all possible bargains at a pitiful price. "I do not believe there is a spot where peace can be found," he says to us, "except under the shadow of the Cross." [52] And those who buy of him never appear to regret it. Pain, anguish, and fear, hell and sin and all their concomitants are shaken off and fade away and vanish. And if you will not believe Moody himself, listen to William James, who had studied the process of salvation carefully, as a philosopher, from the outside, but with the closest scrutiny: "There is a state of mind known to religious men, but to no others, in which the will to assert ourselves and hold our own has been displaced by a willingness to close our mouths and be as nothing in the floods and waterspouts of God. In this state of mind, what we most dreaded has become the habitation of our safety, and the hour of our moral death has turned into our spiritual birthday. The time for tension in our soul is over, and that of happy relaxation, of calm deep breathing, of an eternal present, with no discordant future to be anxious about, has arrived. Fear is not held in abeyance as it is by mere morality, it is positively expunged and washed away." [53]

The passionate, transforming, transfiguring glory of Moody's conception is summed up in the magnificent line of Marlowe:

"See how Christ's blood streams in the firmament!"

And no doubt to some of us such symbolization seems remote and even barbaric. Unfortunately to many of these persons heaven and hell and Christ and even God will seem remote also. But there is one thing that is not remote, and that is death. You may run or ride away from it. You may try to forget it, or hide it with flowers, or with adjectives, or with theories. But death is there, just the same, one indisputable fact in a universe of doubt, death with all its burden of haunting, tormenting, eternal, inevitable question. Moody's answer to that question may or may not have present and permanent validity; but I do not know that the ages have found any more comforting or satisfying.

CHAPTER III

MOODY THE PREACHER

I

MOODY was most himself, most eagerly and energetically alive, when he stood up before a vast expectant audience to pour out in darting, stinging, animating words his gospel of the cleansing blood of Christ. The excitement and enthusiasm of this process seem to have effected a striking change in his manner and appearance. If you passed him in the street, he looked heavy, stolid, his neckless head sunk between his thick shoulders, his full dark beard putting out expression, his gross bulk of cumbering flesh certainly not suggesting any peculiar illumination by the radiance of spirit. An observer, who to be sure exaggerated some points, says of him: "When he is at rest, no person could well seem more uninteresting or vacant. His face is neither pleasant nor attractive, his eye dead and heavy, his figure short and thickset, his bodily presence weak and his speech contemptible."[1] But the same observer dwells upon these duller elements only to emphasize the change

99

that took place when the right influences were at work. "The presence of a multitude has the power to transfigure the man and he becomes for the time another person." [2] Every one agrees about this. The sense that he was to deliver the message that inspired his whole being to even one auditor, and far more to a vast, listening, quivering assembly put glory in his eyes, fire upon his tongue, and impressiveness, even dignity into his weighty and somewhat cumbrous movements.

It is evident that the gift of preaching came to Moody by instinct and force of nature, since he had none of the training or discipline of the regularly taught and prepared minister. There is no particular sign of his at any time making a study of public speaking as an art. He began by talking naturally to his Sunday-School class, because he had something to say, and he kept it right up in the same vein and spirit to the end. Of course his intense keen shrewdness of attention and observation profited by every sermon that he heard, and he was always on the watch to seize a man's merits and to avoid his defects. No doubt, as he was much influenced by Dr. Kirk's doctrine, so he got something of manner from him, though Kirk was far more formal. Moody may also have been influenced by Evans, who had Moody's homely vigor of illustration, though far more sweep of imaginative touch. But probably no man ever gained more by letting his own passionate impulse speak through him. He would have expressed the essential secret of his message much as Finney did: "When I came to preach the Gospel, my mind was so anxious to be thoroughly understood that I studied in the most earnest manner, on the one hand to avoid what was vulgar and on the other to express my thoughts with the greatest simplicity of language."[3] In any event Moody never hesitated to declare his contempt for the artificial element in preaching, for those who make the manner all, for labored rhetoric and the search for fine language for itself. "If God has given you a message," he says, "go and give it to the people as God has given it to you. It is a stupid thing to try to be eloquent."[4]

As to the preparation of his sermons, it should be understood that he usually, if not always, spoke without notes. No one understood better than he the importance of having the eye right on the audience every minute, of not letting any least flutter of effect of any kind escape. He knew also the advantage of not being tied to written words, of letting the splendor of the Holy Spirit whirl him whither it would. No one would have appreciated more fully the words of Whitefield: "After I had begun, the Spirit of the Lord gave me freedom, till at length it came down like a mighty rushing wind, and carried all before it." [5]

At the same time he prepared his sermons with the greatest care. Appearing, as he did, before such very different audiences, the substance could be repeated over and over again, and he did repeat it without fear, to an extent that makes continuous reading of his printed volumes a little monotonous. Nevertheless, he was always developing, elaborating, modifying. He gathered notes from every direction, from his reading, from the newspapers, from everything he saw and heard, and all this new material was skillfully woven into the original fabrics, so that he contrived to give an extraordinary impression of freshness, even to those who had heard him often. And this impression was deepened and strengthened by the intensity with which he felt everything himself before he passed it on to others. Note his answer when asked how he prepared his sermon on the compassion of Christ: "I took the Bible and began to read it over to find out what it said on that subject. I prayed over the texts as I went along until the thought of His infinite compassion overpowered me, and I could only lie on the floor of my study, with my face in the open Bible, and cry like a little child." [6] A man who felt his work like that and could impart his feeling to others could hardly fail to move them.

As to the preacher's manner and delivery opinions differ according to their source. Probably as harsh a verdict as any is that given by the utterly unsympathetic critic of the London Saturday Review: "As for Mr. Moody, he is simply a ranter of the most vulgar type. . . . It is possible that his low fun and screechy ejaculations may be found stimulating by the ignorant and foolish; but it is difficult to conceive how any person of the slightest culture or refinement can fail to be pained and shocked." [7] These severe judgments are, however, rarely echoed by unprejudiced critics, and what foundation there may have been for them diminished with years and experience. In spite of his intense earnestness, it is generally insisted that Moody's manner was restrained and his impetuous fire always under control. There was nothing whatever of the excesses of speech that have recently distinguished Billy Sunday. "He was intense in spirit," says Dr. Abbott, "but quiet in method, generally conversational in tone, never shouted, rarely was dramatic, never theatrical, his gestures simple." [8] His voice had not exceptional beauty or richness, but it had extraordinary carrying power, so that he could fill enormous auditoriums without appearing to force it in the least and while still retaining full command of all its variations of expression. In the same way he used an astonishing rapidity of utterance, resembling and fully equaling Phillips Brooks in that respect; yet he never fretted or fatigued his audience by this quality, simply gave the sense of a splendid abundance which could not be exhausted.

As to the merely technical, linguistic character of the sermons as printed, they have seemed to me far above what one would expect from much of the criticism. The savage Unitarian author of "Tabernacle Sketches" cries, "Oh, the way that man does mangle the English tongue! The daily slaughter of syntax at the Tabernacle is dreadful. His enunciations may be pious, but his pronunciations are decidedly off color. It is enough to make Noah Webster turn over in his grave and weep to think that he lived in vain." [9] No doubt English grammar is handled in a rough and ready and rather colloquial fashion. But the important point is that the language gets there. It is amazingly simple, direct, and vivid. The words are for the most part rugged Anglo-Saxon. The sentences are short. Dr. Goss estimates that in various passages of about 530 words chosen from different preachers, Moody uttered thirty-six sentences, Spurgeon twenty-one, Bushnell twenty, Chalmers nine.[10] In fact, his language was that of daily life, and the common people heard him gladly, and so did some others.

As to the structure of the sermons, they were not elaborate or artful. Perhaps they were all the more effective on that account. There was no attempt to work up a process of extensive logical argument. The preacher got a thorough hold of his subject. Then he chose topics that would develop it, sometimes cumulatively, sometimes by contrast, and handled them one by one with direct vividness of appeal, so as to bring the whole home to his auditors. Above all, he understood the cardinal principal of brevity. To be sure, people sometimes wondered at his flow of words. But he always gave the impression that there was more behind than the words would carry. And he knew when to stop. In sermons, and especially in prayers, he believed in being short. "I say five minutes, some pray fifteen minutes; I don't know any meeting that can stand that. If you can't pray short, don't pray at all. The men who make long prayers are generally the ones that pray least at home." [11]

With this disposition, it would not be expected that Moody's sermons would be marked by any very striking qualities of imagination or poetry. There are indeed times when the emotion rises to a pitch that may be called distinctly poetical. For instance, there is the description of the Flood: "God did not permit any one to survive to tell us how they perished. When Job lost his family, there came a messenger to him; but there came no messenger from the antediluvians; not even Noah himself could see the world perish. If he could, he would have seen men and women and children dashing against that ark; the waves rising higher and higher, while those outside were perishing, dying in unbelief. Some think to escape by climbing the trees, and think the storm will soon go down; but it rains on, day and night, for forty days and forty nights, and they are swept away as the waves dash against them. The statesmen and astronomers and great men call for mercy;

but it is too late. They had disobeyed the God of mercy. He had called, and they refused. He had pled with them, but they had laughed and mocked. But now the time is come for judgment instead of mercy." [12]

But in general Moody's strength does not lie in ornament or in imaginative effects of any kind. It is rather in his intense, direct, immediate appeal to the simplest, the most permanent, the most compelling emotions. The sharp, rude, energetic vigor with which he makes this appeal must have been almost irresistible, when accompanied by his commanding tone and personality. It is true that the vigor has at times a startling touch of the familiar, which might well shock those accustomed to the more staid and conventional manner of formal preachers. Moody speaks of God and to God as if He were a man around the corner, who could be addressed and touched like a real human friend. But it must be remembered that this was much the manner of the Middle Ages also, and it is a serious question whether real reverence has gained greatly by the enormous added remoteness with which later centuries have clothed and perhaps buried the Divine Presence. We have become so intensely reverent, so afraid of humanizing Deity, that at times it seems as if we tended to revere God out of existence altogether. Such was not Moody's way. His God was nothing if not real, a direct human agency, who could be brought right into the immediate joys and sorrows of life. To him love was, as it always should be, far more than reverence, or rather the reverence that was built on close and immediate love was the only reverence that was of serious account.

And speaking with this direct, familiar power, there is no doubt but that he often got descriptions and narratives of a high dramatic intensity, narratives which kept his hearers fixed with eager anticipation or thrilled with hope or terror till they forgot him and themselves and where they were and all their ordinary life in the overwhelming preoccupation of the things of the future and the things of God. But I think the best observers agree that in getting these dramatic moments Moody did not give the impression, either at the time or afterwards, of being melodramatic or sensational, and the obvious reason was that, as we have seen, he himself felt profoundly first everything that he was trying to convey. The heart, he cried, always go for the heart, speak to that, preach to that, if you want to carry men with you. He carried men with him because he preached to the heart and from the heart.

One of the most effective elements of Moody's preaching was his power of illustration, of turning the incidents and experiences of daily life into apt arguments to push home his points. It is said that he was always on the look-out for bits of this kind and picked them from every sort of source. "With what keenness he listened to other preachers for good thoughts and illustrations, and how his face lit up as he took out the notebook which he kept in his hip-pocket." [13] And his adventures in life were so vast and varied, he came into contact with so many people of all kinds, people who opened their hearts to him as they did to few others, that his memory gradually became a storehouse of material which he could put to the most varied and effective use. To be sure, I think the limits show here as in other things, and the mere variety of illustration is not so great as one might expect. What counts is the mighty, homely force of it, the singular power of turning a platitude into a patitude by connecting it with some experience which the hearer feels to be plucked right out of his own soul.

But, after all, perhaps the fundamental secret

of Moody's preaching lay mainly in the fact that he stood up before thousands and spoke to them simply as man to man. He himself tells the story: "Let me say right here that I like to say 'to speak' better than 'to preach,' because if I can only get people to think I am talking with them, and not preaching, it is so much easier to hold their attention. The other night I was walking home in the dark, and two people right behind me were talking about the meeting. One of them said, 'Did Moody preach to-night?' The other said, 'No, he didn't preach, he only talked.'"[14] If that simple motto could be written over the doors of the theological schools, it might help them to change the world.

II

But, preaching or talking, it is evident that words were the main agency that Moody used to arouse, to stimulate, to make over, perhaps to save, thousands of souls. Words were the supreme, practically the only, weapon in his armory, as in that of all other preachers since the beginning of time. And one is lost in astonishment when one reflects upon the power of these diminutive puffs of breath, power which lies sometimes in the vast suggestion of thought they carry with them, but sometimes also, alas, in the mere intonation, the music, the resonance of the voice that puts them forth.

Words are and must be the chief medium of contact between soul and soul, so far as such contact is possible at all. For the mysterious and fleeting entity which we call soul is so remotely immured in these involving, separating bodies, that any real contact escapes us until those who reflect feel themselves isolated in a shuddering solitude which no effort can bridge or overcome. No doubt we can penetrate the mask a little by the aid of expression and gesture. But the only real means we have of even attempting to make our way under it is by the medium of speech. The lesson of the moving pictures is most fruitful and significant on this point. The cruder, more violent, more primitive emotions and situations can be suggested on the screen with poignant intensity. But all the finer grades and shades of spiritual experience seem to cry out for speech and to perish from a pitiful dumb incapacity to convey the straining of life to life.

Words are logical vehicles, by which one man conveys to another his more or less elaborate processes of thought. A man works out a system of reasoning which, as it seems to him, is bound to change the social conditions of the world, to overthrow the tyrannous dominion of capital and enable all mankind to enjoy the fruits of their labor in equalized content. He puts quick and vivid words to his theory and thousands catch it up and shake the social fabric with a vague unrest. Words are emotional vehicles. A man's soul burns with love and hate, alas, more often hate, and if he has the gift of words, he can make his love or hate spread with a wide wave motion to the end of the world. Few things show the power of words more than their capacity for boredom. An empty head with a tongue that quivers with words can take you by the sleeve and make life seem an impossible thing. A great audience gathers, full of enthusiasm and eagerness, ready to be carried off its feet by one who knows words in all their magic. Instead, the conventional orator gets up, pours out his flood of nothing, and all the enthusiasm melts away and like enough the audience also.

It would be easy to maintain that words are the greatest power in the world. They are mighty with individuals, they can undermine friendship, they can break off love, they can wear out even the most divine patience, and when you look for the huge cause of all the trouble, you find it to be just ill-managed words. They are mighty with nations. Thrones have been wrecked, governments have crumbled to pieces, hearts have been broken and heads cut off, only for words. What is most terrifying is that the power of words is not necessarily greatest in the wise, in those who best understand the use of them. The ignorant, the prejudiced, the shallow have often a cunning sleight of speech which sways the vulgar at their will, when the skilled and the thoughtful, who should lead, cannot find their way at all. Take the strange force of abstract words, to which no two persons attach the same definite meaning. Take Liberty. As Madame Roland said, What crimes have been committed under that name. Yet those who shriek most wildly for liberty have each a different interpretation of it. Take the greatest of all words, God. Men in all ages have derived from those three little letters, or their equivalent, the greatest ecstasy. Over and over men have fought and bled and died for those letters. Yet who will fix a meaning for them that men will not fight over, and some persons maintain that they have no meaning except in the subjective associations which have such a mighty hold on almost all of our lives. Truly, one who has played with words and worked with them and felt the charm of them hardly knows which to admire most, their appalling power or their emptiness.

It is curious, too, to note that words have an especial magic and fascination for those who have not been highly or carefully trained in the use of them. The most interesting illustration of this is Shakespeare. With his excitable imagination, his eager and attentive ear, it is evident that he was extraordinarily quick to catch the use of words about him; but neither among his contemporaries nor anywhere else in literature does there seem to have been any one who had such intense delight in words as playthings, who so loved to mold them, to bend them, to create them, as it were, out of nothing, and make them do his will even to the most fantastic ends. Or a somewhat similar case is our own American Whitman, who was irregularly trained like Shakespeare and like him loved to make daring, bewildering, complex experiments with words.

And Moody was as untrained as Shakespeare and Whitman were. And, like them, he loved to do great things with words. But words were never toys to him. They were clubs, they were slings, they were arrows, with which to go out and do battle against the clinging, overmastering evil of the world. As to any slightest consciousness of the nature of words, their power, their danger, or their working, I have found no evidence of it in him whatever. He took them as they came and was simply interested in what he could make them do. How they did it was not in the least his concern. No doubt, in this as in other things, his ignorance was his force, and by accepting these mighty, winged, subtle, intangible agents unquestioningly, he was enabled to get more out of them than if he had understood their fragility. At any rate, no one can question what he did get. Shakespeare could weave them together for the delight of millions. Moody could pour them out so that thousands had their souls stirred and shaken by them like leaves in an autumn wind.

III

Now let us look a little more closely into the character of the audiences to which he preached and the way he affected them. To begin with, from the time of his first real success in the early seventies, the audiences were always large, immense, and he liked it so, would have it so. He was at his best with a throng and he did not propose to speak to fewer if he could help it. The numbers ran usually into the thousands, sometimes to ten thousand or more, and he somehow contrived to make them hear him, or think they heard him, to make them feel him at any rate. To be sure, it is said that in later years he deliberately tried to break up these multitudes, to divide them for more immediate effect. But to the very end he could draw an immense crowd when he chose. On his last visit to Chicago he insisted on having the meetings in the busiest part of the working day. Dr. Torrey explained to him that men were too much engaged to come at that hour, but Moody bade him do as he was told, and Torrey went ahead with some misgiving; "When the doors were opened at the appointed time, we had a cordon of twenty policemen to keep back the crowd, but the crowd was so great that it swept the cordon of policemen off their feet and packed eight thousand people into the building before we could get the doors shut. And I think there were as many left on the outside as there were in the building." [15]

In such a vast number there naturally were

MOODY'S TABERNACLE.

First building erected after Chicago fire. Occupied for two years. A scene of remarkable evangelistic effort.

ILLINOIS STREET CHURCH, CHICAGO.

First building erected by Mr. Moody. Scene of his efforts before Chicago fire.

D. L. MOODY.

From a portrait in oil by Healey. The one relic saved by Mrs. Moody from the
Chicago fire.

people of all sorts. There were people of high intelligence, there were people of low intelligence. There were many who went from mere curiosity or even animosity, and some who went to make a careful study of an important psychological phenomenon. Perhaps in some corner, or even right down in the front, we might have found our ubiquitous Shakespearean clown, impervious to soul-appeals because he had no soul or had all soul, but quick to feel the wide and varied laughter and pity of the world. And it seems that Moody's power touched almost all of them in some way sooner or later. An astonishing number of those who came to scoff remained to pray. Yet, it is probable that the bulk of Moody's audiences everywhere were men and women something of his own kind, church members, or people with church connections or associations, who were instinctively drawn to that form of excitement or entertainment. An excellent observer makes this remark about the congregations of Billy Sunday: "The first thing that strikes one on entering Sunday's tabernacle is that there is an extraordinary homogeneity of the audience. . . . Scrutinize them as carefully as one may, they display a like-facedness that never ceases to be a source of wonder to the perspicuous sympathetic onlooker, and the more their conduct is observed, the more one becomes convinced of their like-mindedness." [16] It should be remembered that almost any average assembly gives such an impression of homogeneity. Furthermore I imagine that Moody's audiences were far more varied than those here analyzed. Still, he himself complained that his popularity with the religious masses prevented his getting to the people he most desired to reach: "I am not blind to facts, nor troubled with mock humility. Reputation is a great injury in many places, for we cannot get the people that we are after." [17]

However his audiences were composed, there is no doubt as to his power of managing them when he had once got them before him. After all practical explanations of this power have been offered, it sometimes seems as if there must have been some mysterious magnetic influence which could enable one man, and he not the most imposing in appearance, to control so absolutely such enormous multitudes. But to some extent it is possible to understand the skillful methods that he employed. Very likely he never heard of crowd psychology or of the epidemic suggestibility of masses of people, but his practical appreciation of these things was perfect. There must be nothing disturbing, nothing out of accord with the spirit that he was trying to use and infuse. If any spectator sought to take an offensive part, to introduce noise or confusion, the ushers were trained to dispose of him with the least possible disturbance The preacher studied the conditions with the utmost care. People would not listen unless they were comfortable. The room must not be too hot, it must not be too cold. There must be plenty of fresh air, yet no one must be exposed to drafts. He looked out for all these things, or saw that they were looked out for. Then he had no heavy formality, no pompous professional manner. Dr. Abbott emphasizes this: "As he stood on the platform he looked like a business man; he dressed like a business man; he took the meeting in hand as a business man would; he spoke in a business man's fashion." [18] And he planned every detail so that there should be no break, no dragging, no slightest occasion or excuse for a yawn. "From the time he came before his great audiences to the moment when he rose to preach he kept the entire body absorbingly occupied with something interesting." [19]

It is curious to note the quickness and skill with

which he took advantage of every incident or accident that occurred while he was preaching, and turned it from a hindrance into a help. If there was an interruption of any kind, he used it to point a moral. Once a lost child turned up in the audience and began to wail. Moody held it up before the crowd and called out, "A lost child! A lost child!" until the mother appeared. Then he proceeded to bring home to the multitude that they were all lost children and could only be found again through the agency of Christ. One of his secrets in dealing with such vast assemblies was to point his talk directly at an individual, in such a way that every one present felt that the individual meant him or her. "I always select a few people in the audience here and there, to whom I speak. If I can interest them and hold their attention, I have the entire audience. If any one of these goes to sleep or loses interest, I work to secure the attention of that one." [20] He thrust his "Are you a Christian?" into sleepy faces, till they had to make him an answer. The suddenness, the startling directness, of these appeals made them piquant and telling to everybody. "I wish that friend over there would just wake up, and I'll tell him something which is important to him." [21] He would

call out to this red-headed man, or that chattering
girl. All at once the man and the girl found the
attention of thousands turned to them, and it woke
up them and the audience both.

There is abundant evidence as to the effect produced by these and other ingenious methods and
devices, backed and sustained as they always were
by the passionate earnestness and enthusiasm
which were more than any device. It is easy to
suppose that Moody might have equaled the violent hysterical tumults of his predecessors, if he
had chosen to do so. His effects were of the spirit,
but, as he willed, he could draw forth the shudder
of spiritual terror and still more the acme of
spiritual joy. Dr. Goss says of this influence:
"There were certain passages in some of his sermons where, judged by the effect they produced, it
must be said he rose to a sublime eloquence. I
heard him preach his sermon on 'Elijah' in the
city of Detroit, when it appeared to me that super-
natural things were actually occurring in the
room. The line of demarcation between the real
and the imaginary seemed broken down. . . . The
excitement was almost unendurable." [22] But I like
best Moody's own quiet comment, with its little
humorous touch of intentional sophistry: "What

we want is preaching for effect. Some people say, 'Oh, that sermon is all preached for effect.' Of course it is; that is what we want, to wake people up." [23] If effect was what he wanted, he got it.

IV

But what interests me most of all is not his effect upon his audiences, but their effect upon him. The psychology of those who work directly in immediate presence upon multitudes of men is of profound significance, at any rate to one who feels that love and glory are the only two things that approach making existence endurable, the tragedy of existence being that love is something we cannot keep and glory something we cannot get. The writer, the painter, the sculptor work mainly in solitude and the echo of glory comes to them dimmed and obscured by distance and reflection. The public performer, whether preacher or orator or actor or singer or prize fighter, gets his glory direct, immediate, in huge, intoxicating doses, mingled with immediate bitter, which often induces jealousy and anger and despair. He acts consciously upon his public and his public reacts upon him with a quick, intense excitement, which is hardly equaled by any other upon earth, except that of actual physical conflict. This psychology has not, I think, been studied so widely as it might be; but the difficulty of the study is no doubt increased by the fact that the objects of it are not usually of a temperament to help us very much themselves. Prize fighters and baseball players are not inclined to be introspective, and it is doubtful whether actors and musicians are much more so. To be sure, there is a good deal to be gleaned from the memoirs of the actor, Macready; and shreds and snatches may be picked up elsewhere by those who care to look for them. I like especially the account of Charlotte Cushman's experience, when she returned to the stage after a prolonged absence. "Just then the storm of applause burst out afresh for a second 'call'; as Miss Cushman heard it, she threw up her arms with a peculiar gesture and cried out in a tone of indescribably passionate eager ecstasy, 'Oh, how have I lived without this through all these years!' " [24]

In the case of the actor and the athlete, however, the desire of glory and personal success is openly the object. Every one expects such persons to live for applause and to admit it. The case of the preacher or the social reformer is complicated by his professing to eschew glory altogether, to work for the benefit of others, and to regard popularity and success as merely incidental and only of importance as indicating that he is doing his work and doing it well. It is just this that makes the peculiar fascination of the problem. Preachers are human. Applause and glory have always appealed to them, and always will. "The vanities of all others may die out, but the vanity of a saint as regards his sainthood is hard indeed to wear away," says one who spoke from experience.[25] To disentangle such an obscure web of motives is as delightful as it is difficult. No lover of human nature will turn from the task. As Sainte-Beuve puts it, "Let us not be afraid to surprise the human heart naked, in its incurable duplicity, even in the saints." [26]

Even in the saints ambition and the desire for glory are evident enough, and sometimes admitted. Have we not the confession of General Booth, after he was converted? "Have you no ambition? Because I have, I intend to do something great; I don't mean to belong to the commonalty." [27] And we can watch the cruder desire turning into the subtler impulse, when he writes later: "I wanted to be right with God. I wanted to be right in myself. I wanted a life spent in putting other people right." [28]

The saints are well enough aware of the danger of this love of applause, excitement, and success. "The charm of glory is so great," says Pascal, "that we love it no matter what it may attach itself to, even to death." [29] Saint Augustine feels the doubt and the difficulty: "If praise is the natural adjunct of good life and good works, then we should not avoid the adjunct any more than the things themselves." [30] Whitefield proclaims hardily and vividly the incurable passion for the wandering preacher's life: "This itch after itinerating I hope will never be cured till we come to heaven." [31] Again, "Let me enjoy myself in my delightful itineracy. It is good both for my body and soul." [32] Or the passion will display itself in strange, inverted forms. After all, perhaps the greatest testimony of the revivalist's success is the tumult he creates among the powers of evil. As one of the early American workers delightfully expresses it: "I knew in all probability hell was in an uproar." [33] Even more delightful is the experience of Finney with the devil-possessed horse. He asks the young man who is going to drive him if the horse is safe. "Because, if the Lord wants me to go to Stephentown, the devil will prevent it if he can; and if you have not a steady horse, he will try to make him kill me." To complete the narrative: "Strange to tell, before we got there, the horse ran away twice, and came near killing us. His owner expressed the greatest astonishment, and said he had never known such a thing before." [34] Could you find a more charming illustration of enlargement of the ego than measuring its importance by the attentions of the devil? "Let us not be afraid to surprise the human heart naked, in its incurable duplicity, even in the saints."

V

In considering Moody's career from this point of view of applause, success, and popularity, we must first of all establish the essential earnestness, modesty, humility, and self-effacement of the man, at any rate so far as his own consciousness was concerned. No one knew better than he the insinuating, engrossing power of the I, its overmastering dominance when allowed to have its way, and no one fought it with more energy, in others and in his own heart. He once rebuked in a public meeting a brother evangelist who complained bitterly of the opposition he had met. "I can tell you, sir, why they opposed you," said Moody. "Why?" "Because you spoke too much about yourself." [35] He did not propose to speak or to think too much about himself, if he could help it. Again and again he attacks the I, scourges it, declares that it should be cast out relentlessly: "One of the truest signs that a man is growing great is that God increases and he decreases. Why, some people will talk about themselves by the yard. 'I, I, I, I.' There will be forty-nine I's in a speech five minutes long." [36] And elsewhere: "This is the age of boasting. It is the day of the great 'I'." [37] He gives a vivid picture of the struggle of the I in himself, a passionate struggle in which he felt that in the end the I was completely overcome: "For four long months God seemed to be just showing me myself. I found I was ambitious; I was not preaching for Christ; I was preaching for ambition. I found everything in my heart that ought not to be there. For four long months, a wrestling went on within me, and I was a miserable man." [38]

The testimony of others to Moody's self-abnegation is more positive and of course far more weighty, than his own. Among the innumerable witnesses I do not know any more emphatic than Dr. Torrey: "Oh, how he loved to put himself in the background and put other men in the foreground. How often he would stand on a platform with some of us little fellows seated behind him and as he spake he would say: 'There are better men coming after me. . . .' I do not know how he could believe it, but he really *did* believe that the others that were coming after him were really better than he was. He made no pretense to a humility he did not possess. In his heart of hearts he constantly underestimated himself and overestimated others. He really believed that God would use other men in a larger measure than he had been used." [39] There is no disputing Dr. Torrey's absolute sincerity, nor Moody's. Yet such a passage affords vast matter for curious reflection, and it is permissible to suggest that some of the greatest egotisms of the world have loved to put others forward with the subtle sense underneath that the putter-forward could do the work and do it better, if he would, or at any rate that he was the master of his substitutes.

Whatever Moody's attitude toward it may have been, there is no doubt of the enormous admira-

tion, laudation, just plain glory that followed him
wherever he went. Great men bowed down to
him, learned men deferred to him, rich men
opened their purses freely. If he would, he
might have had a train of adoring women; but
it is one of the fine things about him that the
adulation of women did not appeal. As Mr.
Duffus puts it: "He never let gushing women
make a fool of him." [40] His success might have
been portrayed as vividly as in the words in which
Whitefield describes his own: "It was wonderful
to see how the people hung upon the rails of the
organ-loft, climbed upon the leads of the church,
and made the church itself so hot with their
breath that the steam would fall from the pillars
like drops of rain." [41] Moody indulges in no such
fatuous narrative, but there can be no doubt that
he was quite well aware what the success was.
It was something to have a man like Henry Drummond announce in print your supremacy on this
earth: "Henry Drummond declared that Mr.
Moody was the greatest man this century had produced." [42] It was even more to have followers so
ecstatic that they could predict an equal supremacy in heaven: "I want to say a word of Mr.
Moody's entrance into heaven. When he entered

into heaven there must have been an unusual commotion. . . . It was a triumphal entrance into glory!" [43]

No doubt Moody dodged the extreme manifestations of this devotion when he could. He was altogether too big to enjoy being pawed over or purred over, or to permit it. An enthusiast promised a great company of "our first ladies" that they should shake hands with the evangelist after a meeting. The evangelist took his hat and the next cab that passed and disappeared. [44] He distrusted flattery, detested it, shrank from it, knew its undermining, debasing power, and was determined not to let it work its subtle way with him. Just after his great triumph in Scotland in 1874, he wrote to a friend: "Pray for me every day; pray now that God will keep me humble." [45]

The nature of the prayer and its earnestness show an obscure and constant sense of the danger; but the man's external preoccupations were so constant and his aversion to analysis so great that he was probably hardly aware of the complicated nature of the spiritual processes that agitated his soul. Of course he enjoyed freely, lavishly, the stimulus, the intense and varied excitement that his chosen calling afforded. Think of the contrast between what he began with and what he became: a little, ignorant, neglected, routine shoe-clerk, and then the absolute arbiter of thousands of destinies for this world and another. To get up before those vast audiences, take them in the hollow of your hand, and swing them up to heaven by the mere power of your breath, what other delight in life could surpass it? He himself tells us that "the richest hours I have ever had with God have not been in great assemblies like this, but sitting alone at the feet of Jesus." [46] I have no doubt that he makes the statement with absolute veracity, but I question its truth, all the same. Or rather, if those hours were the richest, there were others that were more magnificent. Not receptive quiet, but turbulent activity was his atmosphere: "He seems to be always carried along on a sea of inspiration. He passes his life tossing on its waves, where he is as perfectly at home as the stormy petrel on the ocean." [47]

It was not only that he had the excitement of the ordinary established popular preacher, with the same great city audience daily at his feet. This man roved over the world trailing crowds behind him. Not for him were the drudgeries of the settled pastor, the parish squabbles, the parish poor.

He had none of the burdens or obligations of the minister regularly ordained. His share was none of the labors and all the fun. There was a charm in the very perpetual movement of it, new scenes, new faces, new souls, new problems. Says the ancient analyst: "For peregrination charms our senses with such unspeakable and sweet variety that some count him unhappy that has never traveled, a kind of prisoner, and pity his case, that from his cradle to his old age beholds the same; still, still, still the same." [48] But with the evangelist the mere charm of peregrination was tripled by the splendor of doing the will of God and sweeping souls into his kingdom. The extraordinary spiritual dangers involved in this are well indicated by a sympathetic student of revivals generally: "The proof is conclusive that the itinerant revivalist is in peculiar danger. As he naturally soon leaves a place where he is unsuccessful, he spends most of his time where his own power over the minds of men is the most conspicuous object in his sight and where he is delighted with the proofs of his own eminent influence. . . . He has abundant reason to know with Whitefield 'how difficult it is to meet success and not be puffed up with it,' and to say with him,

'My corruptions are so strong and my employment so dangerous that I am sometimes afraid.'"[49]

Moody's steady head and quiet heart through all this turmoil are astonishing and indisputable. But there is much to reflect upon in the account of a little talk with him given by a friend: "On the way to a prayer-meeting that I knew would be crowded, though held in a large church, I remarked to him, 'You must experience great pleasure in going from place to place, and reaching and benefiting such multitudes as come to hear you.' He seemed scarcely to know what to say. He could not deny that he was engaged in a delightful work, but his whole mind seemed to be upon the work rather than upon his personal relations to it. I cannot recall precisely his reply. But the distinct impression left upon my mind was that this man thinks of nothing, plans for nothing but for Christ and souls."[50] The curious analytical considerations that this suggests are best supplemented and completed by the simple sentence of Moody's biographer, "public services had become a second nature to him."[51]

The keen and constant enjoyment of his daily tasks was heightened in Moody's case by the singular absence of any real doubt or self-mistrust.

D. L. MOODY: A WORKER IN SOULS

Not for him were the agonies of question that afflicted a Pascal or even a Wesley or a Booth. He tells of moments of discouragement, but they are so rare that they prove the rule. Speaking broadly, it may be said that from beginning to end his career was one of joyous, exalted, exhilarated success.

In other words, we have an ego so big, so expansive, that it could not be inflated to damage or injury, but filled to its capacity with the sense of creative power, the intensest intoxicant known to man, and filled from the most inexhaustible reservoir, the belief that God was behind it. Can there be on earth a more positive, enthralling assertion of the ego than the "belief that God has singled out D. L. Moody for a great work," [52] and that belief was always and steadily Moody's. There is no evidence that long and yearning ambition was consciously prominent in him, because he was not a widely imaginative man, and the immense, unfailing fulfillment kept him well ahead of anything he could dream of. But how he did enjoy himself. When his son says of him that he "lived solely for the glory of God and for the spread of the Gospel of Jesus Christ," [53] the proposition is in a sense perfectly true. But living for God, as he did it, is surely about the greatest amusement and self-satisfaction that life can afford.

Yet no one can dwell with Moody long without being convinced that he would have thrown over all his glory and success in a moment, if he had been convinced that God willed it. It is said that in later years he deliberately changed his methods, dividing his audiences in a way to yield less personal triumph for himself, but greater results.[54] I have no doubt it is true. And we may go further. I wrote once of Frances Willard that if you could have persuaded her that it was her duty to give up all her public activity and notoriety and devote herself to humble personal charitable work in some obscure corner, she would have done it without a moment's hesitation. So there is no doubt that if you could have persuaded Moody that it was God's will that he should relinquish his larger labors and go as a missionary to the Labrador fishermen or even settle down as an insignificant pastor in a country parish, he would have done it at once. But you would have had to be something of a logical expert to persuade him.

VI

One of the definite elements of Moody's triumph and success was the contrast between his eager and enthusiastic congregations and the lukewarmness of the regular churches. No doubt this was partly owing to the peculiar and temporary nature of his appeal. But the lukewarmness was already marked, even in his day, as compared with a hundred years earlier, and it will hardly be denied that it has much increased since. In spite of intelligent and well-directed efforts in social lines, philanthropic lines, and recently in lines of so-called religious education, maintaining a large body of those nominally affiliated with the church, the general influence and power of Protestant churches in the community is far different from what it was in the eighteenth century or in the early nineteenth. The various complicated causes of this condition need hardly be analyzed here. One of the most important was inherent in Protestantism from the Reformation, the emphasis on individual judgment in religious matters. The natural result of this emphasis was the sermon, and the sermon has been the great blight upon the Protestant church. A few brilliant preachers can always hold large audiences in the cities. But to expect the average minister to be original in matter and attractive in delivery is obviously to expect the impossible. As a consequence, the hungry sheep look up and are not fed, and they slink away to seek their nourishment elsewhere.

Another most important cause of the deterioration of church influence, a cause which has already grown up so insidiously and gradually that it is generally overlooked, is the development of journalism. The newspaper, in the popular sense, is the child of the later nineteenth century, and it has certainly changed the world, and most certainly the churches. In early New England the minister was the ruling force in the community. What his power was and how splendidly conscious he was of it appears in the anecdote of a visitor who called upon a country parson and found him digging in his garden. The visitor, a little doubtful as to the state of things, inquired timidly, "Do you serve here?" The parson drew himself up to his full august six feet, and answered, "I rule here." [55]

It was not only that the minister guided his flock religiously. The church was the intellectual center. Men met there to learn by word of mouth the doings of the great world. Now print has changed all that. Social life is not the source of knowledge, but solitude. The newspaper links together communities, but it separates individuals. In the age of Shakespeare, or the age of Jonathan Edwards, education and information were gathered from human contact: if you wished to know what had happened, you asked your neighbor. To-day men ride to their business side by side, and, instead of exchanging news, they both bury themselves in the sporting or the financial or the editorial column. Most of all, in the last fifty years, the Sunday newspaper has been the deadly enemy of the church. It not only gives an excuse for staying at home; but, whereas a hundred years ago, if you wanted to know the movement of politics and finance and society, you had to go to church, now, if you want to know these things, you have to stay at home. Nothing marks this more clearly than the altered position of the minister. He not only no longer rules, he finds it difficult even to serve. The average business man looks upon him with amused patronage. Of course he is not expected to be any more than a child in practical affairs; but even his views on general subjects are regarded as those of a cloudy idealist—or a woman.

Naturally at all times preachers of Moody's genius and power will escape and override this general deterioration, and will find their success emphasized by it. But it is most interesting to see how quickly Moody's keen insight detected the danger in the development of the newspaper and how vigorously and constantly he attacked it. As with everything else, he knew how to use the newspapers for his purpose, when the occasion came. But he mistrusted the enemy, and he did not miss a chance· to express his opinion: "Good Christians are not going to live upon the New York *Ledger*. . . . Do not let us feed upon this new literature, this miserable stuff that is printed." [56]

Especially does he dilate and declaim about the Sunday paper. It is helping more than anything else to undermine the Sabbath: "If you give up the Sabbath, the church goes; if you give up the church the home goes; and if the home goes the nation goes. That is the direction in which we are traveling." [57] He analyzes the Sunday papers and points out their corrupting, debasing, demoralizing influence. It is said that they report sermons. Pooh! Report sermons! He takes a group of seven papers and figures up the contents: "Unclean personals, eight columns, think of a Christian man putting that paper before his children!" etc., etc. And the total is, "Nine hundred and eleven and a quarter columns, and only three and a quarter columns of them religious. That is Sunday reading! Gabriel himself couldn't hold an audience whose heads were full of such stuff as that." [58] When he is told that the fight is hopeless, he replies that the fight of God is never hopeless for him: "They tell me the Sunday paper has come to stay, and I may as well let it alone. Never! I believe it is a great evil, and I shall fight it while I live. I never read a Sunday paper, and wouldn't have one in my house. . . . I will have nothing to do with them. They do more harm to religion than any other agency I know." [59] There is no more pathetic symptom of the fatally losing war that he waged in so many respects than the complete triumph of his journalistic adversaries. They had destiny so wholly on their side that they did not have to notice his attacks.

Within very recent years, however, there has come up another form of publicity which one feels would have been curiously adapted to Moody's purposes, and that is broadcasting by radio. One of the enthusiastic admirers of General Booth, speaking of the eagerness with which he adopted and adapted new instruments, says: "In our day he would have been scouring the skies at the rate of 100 miles an hour, and shouting sermons through the megaphone as he sped." [60] But the radio is a vastly more effective instrument than any megaphone, and already the revivalists of to-day are beginning to make use of it. One can see how it would have appealed to Moody, and how he would have employed it to hurl his "Are you a Christian?" in the faces of millions of idlers all over the world. To be sure, there would have been the loss of corporeal presence, of the stimulating excitement of the visibly absorbed and listening multitude. Yet, after all, Moody wanted to talk to individuals. One can imagine tormented souls, shut off in night and solitude, getting his urgent and insistent appeal through the vibrating air, and overcome with a passionate longing and terror and hope more intense and irresistible than could ever be conveyed in any crowded hall. But the whole business of Moody's dealing with individuals and of his appeal to them will furnish an interesting and important theme for a later chapter.

CHAPTER IV

MOODY AND SANKEY

I

THE influence of music for salvation and damnation both is worthy of careful study and is especially important in dealing with the career of D. L. Moody. In his day the slow, subtle, dreamy magic of the waltz was supposed to whirl thousands of souls into the abyss. And surely he would regard with even more horror the tangled clatter of modern jazz-dancing, with its languid sway of fantastic steps in the naked glare of sex and with the stimulus of intertwining rhythmic motion. Then there is the long enchanting lure of the love-lay through all the ages, teasing restless spirits out of sanity into despair:

> "What is love? 'Tis not hereafter,
> Present mirth hath present laughter,
>   What's to come is still unsure.
> In delay there lies no plenty.
> Then come kiss me, Sweet and Twenty,
>   Youth's a stuff will not endure."

And there is the tinkle of strings with the maddening suggestion of desire and delight across the moonlit waters, only giving place to the more dangerous silence of the stars. Nor is it alone the essentially erotic forms of music that undermine and destroy. In its intensest moments there is often a dissipating, dissolving passion, a haunting, exhilarating, exasperating ardor, which elevates the spirit beyond hope, and then leaves it pale, exhausted, discontented, skeptical, with a grief for which it finds no obtainable remedy and no specific cure.

Yet if music is a mighty agent for damnation, its regenerating power is equally immense and equally wayward and unaccountable. It is not only with the unanimous resonance of great choruses of faith and hope and love that the possession comes, not only with the crash and thunder of huge organs in arched cathedral aisles, though these are often efficacious and irresistible. The song of a veery in a June thicket, the cry of the song sparrow on misty April mornings, the carol of the thrush in August twilights, may fill the heart with a longing that only God can satisfy. A man who is torn and fretted and maddened with the hurrying tumult of the world, who is harassed with the perplexities of business or sick with the satiety of pleasure, may hear a strain of a long-remembered air, perhaps a cadence of a hymn his mother sang to him in childhood, and suddenly the material pressure of the world about him may melt into utter unreality, and he may stand for a moment at least on the threshold of heaven. Now in utilizing these moments and fixing them, in profiting by their subtle secrets of musical association, if not in probing them, Ira David Sankey had a strange, an instinctive, but an undeniable mastery. He did not perhaps adopt Moody's ever-iterated, "Are you a Christian?" in words. But he kept up a tap, tap, tap of melody on the heart which was at times even more effective.

It must be confessed that he did not altogether look the part of a spiritual stimulator, though he looked it more than Moody did. In the case of Moody, indeed, there was a certain charm about the contrast between the heavy, material face and figure and the spiritual message. One of Sankey's enthusiastic admirers compares him to Orpheus.[1] If this is exact, Orpheus must have looked like the average minister, of the less prepossessing type. Sankey's figure was tall and bulky, though dignified. He wore dark, unctuous side whiskers, such as were fashionable in that day, but have now gone out of the world. He was extremely neat and careful as to his clothes, in amusing contrast to the rough-and-ready uncouthness of Moody. Mr. Duffus says that Sankey "looked like the honest proprietor of a meat-market." [2] Another observer records more specifically: "Mr. Sankey weighs about two hundred and twenty pounds avoirdupois, and measures forty-four inches around the chest. This is the weight and chest measure of the *basso profundo* in an opera troupe." [3] And still another adds a few vivid touches: "An immense, bilious man, with black hair, and eyes surrounded by flaccid, pendent, baggy wrinkles, who came forward with an unctuous gesture." [4] But this latter observer, like many others, fell completely under the charm when the music began. It seems that Sankey's singing could transfigure his appearance or make you forget it.

What the man would have been without his voice and without D. L. Moody it is easy to conjecture. He was born in 1840, in a small Pennsylvania town. He was of English and Scotch extraction, but was thoroughly American in most of his characteristics. One rather fatuous biographer informs us that "he was the finest little fellow in the neighborhood." [5] He was probably a boy like many other boys, fairly educated, held under strict discipline, working when he had to, and playing when he got the chance. He served a term in the army during the Civil War and made a success as a singer, if in no other way. Afterwards he was employed in the Government civil service, and seems to have been a quiet, faithful worker. He married a good woman who understood him and he had three children. In short, he was framed to be an average American business man, of sufficiently narrow interests, narrow duties, and narrow pleasures, who would have lived out his sixty odd years in the usual petty insignificance of most of us.

But he had a voice of considerable power, moderate compass, and singularly appealing quality, and he had an extraordinary dramatic instinct in the managing of it. Also, he ran into D. L. Moody just at the fortunate moment. These two things gave him an altogether different career. They brought him out into the great world, trailed him all over the United States and the British Isles, introduced him as an equal and often as a superior to the very greatest people, gave him and his family ease, comfort, and luxury. We read in the *Boston Advertiser,* during the revival in that city: "Mr. Sankey and his family are staying at the Hotel Brunswick." [6] Most notable of all, his singing and his coadjutor brought him praise, admiration, adulation such as fall to few artists of any type. One cannot but be impressed, perhaps even more than with Moody, with what the man might have been, would naturally have been, and what he was. But one fact must be made plain, right at the start: Sankey, like Moody, absolutely refused to make money out of the saving of souls. He was supported by the voluntary contributions of friends and admirers and by moderate payments definitely and legitimately earned. But he did not make any personal gain from the enormous profits received from the "Gospel Hymns." "Mr. Sankey . . . had given up copyrights that would have brought him in a large sum yearly and opportunities to hold musical institutes and conventions which would have added largely to his income." [7] I do not know that there is any much better test of sincerity and devotion.

II

Since Sankey sang for religion and therefore mainly lived for it, it is interesting to know how far religion entered into his own personal life.

Unfortunately with him, as with Moody, there is an irritating lack of really critical information from any competent, unprejudiced source. There is plenty of eulogy, mostly unintelligent, but little scientific analysis. And apparently Sankey, like Moody, was little disposed to analyze himself. I suspect that the singer may have had rather more natural disposition to such work than the preacher. But Moody left a vast verbal outpouring which could not be entirely without self-revelation. Sankey was much less of a talker, at any rate in print. An observer slightly more discriminating than most makes an interesting comparison of the two: "Moody was brusque, but so sincere that any man forgave him. Sankey, on the other hand, was polished, pleasant, sunshiny, in temperament—perhaps, after all, not so easy to fathom as Moody." [8] I cannot make up my mind whether there was less to fathom or whether it was less fathomable.

In any case the man will not help us much. In his autobiographical sketch and elsewhere he tells us more or less of his early religious experiences, not with the slightest suggestion of hypocrisy, but you have the painful sense that he wishes to set a good example to the young. In his childhood he

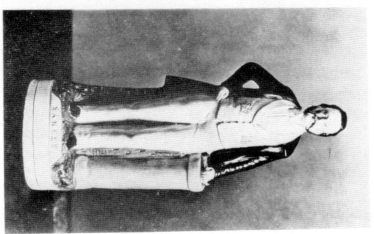

Ira D. Sankey.

was subjected to severe religious discipline: "the boys were not even allowed to whistle on a Sunday." [9] But apparently he did not rebel, rebellion was not in his nature. Even his definite conversion, when it came, was not attended with any unusual delay or recalcitrancy. When he was a youth, "with some young companions he attended a series of special meetings held in a little country chapel, three miles from his father's home, and while sitting in a state of heedlessness and levity, the Spirit of God put it into the heart of an old elder of the church to go and speak to him about his soul. Evening after evening the old man would search him out after the sermon and plead with him to give his heart and consecrate his life to Jesus. Fear of what his young associates would say kept him long from coming to the Cross of Christ. But at last, after a struggle lasting seven days, the experienced elder led him to Jesus." [10] From that time on his religious life seems to have been as sunny and tranquil as could be expected.

Although Sankey's chief usefulness was as a singer, he took more or less general part in the services and as a speaker was by no means ineffective. His voice was pleasant and his manner was easy. He sometimes made impressive and tell-

ing spiritual appeals and he had a humorous turn
which was effective in a lighter line of speaking.
On his last visit to England, he delivered a pleasant farewell address, in which he told of a stranger
who inquired of him what sort of people Moody
and Sankey were: "Just common folks like ourselves," was Sankey's answer. And he explained
his difficulties in making the man believe that he
was not dead.[11] Again, he had a most dramatic
fashion of introducing his hymns. If he was to
sing "The Ninety and Nine," he would tell the
actual story of a prodigal.[12] Here is another instance: "Mr. Sankey said, 'Now is the time for
working. I saw on a tombstone at Stirling yes-
terday this word deeply carved in the stone—
"Waiting." There will be a time for waiting by
and by, but now is the time for *working*.' He then
sang:

> 'Hark, the voice of Jesus crying,
> "Who will go and work to-day?"' "[13]

Also, Sankey had a good deal of gift for dealing with individuals, and in the Inquiry Meetings he was a useful and effective agent. No doubt
his power in this way was much augmented by the
memory and association of his singing. There are

numerous stories of men who came to him and were influenced by him, for instance, that of the atheist lecturer who was converted, as Sankey himself relates in his autobiography,[14] and he seems to have been especially successful with women. Indeed, it would appear that in this respect he surpassed Moody, whose robust and direct methods were perhaps less appealing to the feminine temper. The most severe satirical critic of the evangelists even avers that when Moody took one inquiry room and Sankey the other, Moody had one female out of just one hundred and Sankey ninety-nine.[15] The numbers sound suspicious, but the general proportion may be suggestive. It must be insisted, however, that Sankey, like Moody, was scrupulously careful in such relations, and in all the fierce hostility that prevailed in many quarters I do not find one word of scandal about the singer any more than about his greater friend.

III

It may be said in the main that Sankey's life was in his music, and it is of extreme interest to find out how music affected him—if one only could. He seems to have been fascinated by it from his early days. "I was always fond of singing—it came naturally to me. I sang from childhood, and was literally full and running over with music," he says,[16] and he tells us that when he was eight years old, he could sing correctly such tunes as St. Martin's, Belmont, Coronation, etc.[17] He had apparently very little training, either vocally or instrumentally, but taught himself, by instinct and observation. The influence of the popular religious singer, Philip Phillips, first impressed Sankey with the power and importance of sacred music and induced him to cultivate it with all his energy. But as he had little gift of learning from others, so he was not very skillful at teaching them, and those who went to him in later years to learn his secrets came away unsatisfied.[18]

He had not only early a taste for singing, but for composing. It is said that at "the age of fifteen years he began to compose tunes for his own amusement."[19] Later he composed many of the Gospel Songs, and sang his own music as well as that of others. The general character of these songs, as compared with that of earlier church music, is of course their greater freedom and popularity. The words are often intensely and vividly significant for the singer's purpose, and the melody has a variety, a lightness, sometimes to some ears a flippancy and worldliness, which astonished and shocked and appealed. Sankey often sang the older hymns with power, but his great triumphs were won with music of his own sort. At the same time, some of the most popular and effective of all his pieces seem to have been the hymns of Bliss, "Hold the Fort," "Watching and Waiting," "Pull for the Shore, Sailor." Sankey's own hymns have a little less certainty, a little less poignant directness. There is one exception, however, "The Ninety and Nine," which was as telling as any that he ever sang. Sankey's own story of the composition of this is so significant as to be well worth quoting. He came across the words (by Elizabeth Clephane) in Scotland, but had made no music for them. One day in a meeting Moody called upon him to sing something appropriate to the Good Shepherd. "The impression came upon me, 'Sing the hymn and make the tune as you go along.' It was almost as if I heard a voice, so vivid was the sensation. I yielded to it, and, taking the little newspaper slip and laying it upon the organ before me, with a silent prayer to God for help, I commenced to sing. Note by note, the music was given to me clear through to the end of the tune. After the first verse, I was very glad

I had got through, but overwhelmed with fear that the tune for the next verse would be greatly different from the first. But again looking up to the Lord for help in this most trying moment, He gave me again the same tune for all the remaining verses, note for note. The impression made upon the audience was very deep; hundreds were in tears." [20] This is interesting as showing that, in his composition, as in his singing, Sankey relied less upon scholarly technique or trained discipline, than upon improvisation and inspiration, although he was apt and quick at taking hints from others.

With this evident susceptibility to musical impressions, it would be curious to know how far Sankey was influenced by the greater music of the world, but we get no light at all upon the point. If he ever heard Bach and Mozart and Beethoven and Wagner, or heard of them, we are not told of it. Even oratorio is never mentioned in connection with him. As for opera in any shape, it was of course tabooed with the other iniquities of the theater. Yet closely contemporaneous with Sankey's own triumphs came the equal, if very different triumphs, of Gilbert and Sullivan. One would think that the choruses of the "Pirates" and "Pinafore" and the subtle, passionate melodies of "Patience" and "Iolanthe" would have set the man's heart on fire. Did he hear them? Did he feel them? Who knows? Yet music was always his solace and delight, and in the blindness which came upon him in later days, his refuge and consolation.

Also, he had definite ideas about the use of music for his religious purpose and he very often and very clearly expounded them. Not unnaturally he preferred the voice to instruments. The organ might do well in its place, might have its effect. But he liked a simple reed instrument that could be perfectly subordinated: "I would prefer a small organ near the pulpit and have it played just simply so as not to drown the people's voice, but support them and keep them in tune. It is the human voice we want instead of the playing, for there is nothing equal to the human voice in the world." [21] He believed in solo singing, believed that the words should be made important, significant, and that the tune should be used to wing them to the people's hearts. He wanted the hymn to be adapted to the occasion. He wanted the singers, if they were professional, to be Christians also, to feel what they sang, and not to be mere hired entertainers, who would pass indifferently from the choir-loft, which he disliked, to the opera or concert-stage.

With these views as to religious music, with his native musical ardor, and with his voice, it was fortunate that he found Moody, or that Moody found him.

IV

The value of music for religious services generally and especially for revivals had always been appreciated, but the prominence of solo singing was novel and still more so was the intimate coöperation of preacher and singer. Nothing like it had been known before Moody and Sankey and nothing since has quite equaled their popular reputation. When they came together in 1870, each was feeling his way. Sankey was singing here and there, but was hardly known. Moody was doing his evangelistic work and had all his native gifts, but had still much to learn in practical management. Sankey drifted into a meeting. There was no one to lead the singing, and he took charge. Moody was delighted with his voice and manner and at once seized upon him with characteristic bluntness. "Where do you live?" "In Newcastle, Pennsylvania." "Are you

married?" "Yes." "How many children have
you?" "One." "What are you in business?" "A
revenue officer." "Well, you'll have to give that
up. You are the man I have been looking for this
last eight years. You must give up your business
in Newcastle and come to Chicago. I want you
to help me in my work." [22] The call of Jesus could
hardly have been more arbitrary and more compelling. And Sankey was gently compelled.
After a brief period of hesitation he gave up all
and followed his leader. They worked together
with more and more understanding and effect,
until, in 1873, they departed on the triumphant
progress through the British Isles which established their fame.

It is evident everywhere that Moody was the
bigger and stronger man and dominated Sankey,
as he dominated every one else that came into contact with him, not by violence, but by innate power.
At the very beginning Sankey had an invitation
to go to the Pacific coast with his original model,
Philip Phillips. He hesitated, but Moody prevailed, and Sankey had the insight to choose the
larger spirit with the larger future.[23] He felt the
force and assurance of Moody's guiding genius,
even in matters that pertained more peculiarly to

himself: "Mr. Moody has always been an inspiration to me in preparing hymns for gospel work; not that he was a musician or claimed to be, but I soon learned to prize his judgment as to the value and usefulness of a hymn for our work. What moved him was sure to move others, and what failed to do so could be safely omitted." [24] If Moody said, "You can do it," Sankey felt that he could do it, and he did. In Scotland Moody urged him to use the Scotch dialect. "I realized it was rather a hazardous proceeding to sing a hymn in the vernacular, but Mr. Moody, though he knew. he had put me in a tight place, said, 'Go ahead, Sankey.' I did go ahead, and that was one of the reasons why I and Mr. Moody got on so well during our thirty years' work together." [25] It is even said that it was Moody who persuaded Sankey to give up his royalty on the Hymn Books. However this may be, the influence of the older man in everything is unquestionable. And Sankey not only followed, he loved. After hearing the Moody sermons over and over, with all their unavoidable repetitions, he could say, "I never tired of hearing Mr. Moody speak." [26] In one of his sermons the preacher described the death bed of the unrepentant sinner. Sankey must have heard this many times before, yet he "was visibly affected by the picture, and when he raised his head at the close of the address his eyes were red from weeping." [27] There is surely some test of power in that.

For all his submission, there were times when Sankey could and did assert himself, and it is one of the surest marks of Moody's greatness that he could instantly accept and adopt the suggestions of others when they appealed to his common-sense. On one occasion in a large music-hall Sankey was to sing, but hesitated because he had no organ for his accompaniment. "Isn't that organ enough for you?" asked Moody, pointing to the huge instrument at the back of the platform. Sankey said it was too large and that he could not sing with his back to the audience any more than Moody could preach to them in that way. Moody saw the point, and allowed Sankey to leave the organ out and sing with no accompaniment at all, which he did with his usual success.[28] Sankey also tells us of Moody's prejudice against certain hymns and of the tact necessary to conquer it.[29]

So the two worked along together, overcoming obstacles, pulling through tight places, astonishing vast multitudes, and winning souls. Sometimes Moody's titanic energy was too much for Sankey's more sensitive temperament, and he was forced to trail behind, but in the main he kept going with extraordinary perseverance and success. Not the least attractive part of their intercourse is the exchange of pleasant little jests and quips with which they both diversified even the tumultuous progress of salvation. Speaking in a sermon of Paul's creed, Moody said, "I don't know what Paul's persuasion was. All persuasions claim him. Sankey says he is a Methodist." [30] When Sankey was publicly asked if the leader of a meeting should lead the singing, he replied: "If a singer, he could do it, but of course the man who leads is not always a singer. I think we would have a hard time if I should ask Brother Moody to lead the singing here to-day." A few minutes later he was asked if he recommended solo singing. He answered, "Not as a rule," and Moody interjected, "I would if I had Sankey." [31] And Moody liked to play on Sankey, as on others, the rather primitive sort of practical joke which was mainly his idea of humor. When they were crossing the ferry at Northfield, Moody was helping the ferryman and begged Sankey to sing. "We all thought the crossing very slow. After

the third or fourth song Sankey looked around
and discovered Moody holding on to the wire
and pulling back while the ferryman pulled forward; his object being to get in a good many songs,
not only for his own enjoyment, but for the good
of the ferryman, a boyhood friend for whose conversion he was interested." [32]

As the years went on, the two friends appeared
less frequently together and the association of their
names became more a tradition than a reality.
Moody had somewhat changed his methods of
work. Sankey grew older, and though he still
sang for the Lord, he lived more quietly. Perhaps his voice had not quite its original power,
and his flow of composition may have been less
abundant. I have sometimes wondered whether
the striking words of Dr. Atkins's comment on
Moody's use and disuse of the men who served
him had any remote application to Sankey's case:
"He was the servant of a greater than himself, in
desperate haste about his Master's business; and
the men whom he thrust aside as ill tools knew that
nothing selfish or personal ever directed his action.
They had in his judgment, simply ceased to profit
his Master's cause, and they were willing to be
used by him or discarded by him, because they

had been fired with a like love for the same cause." [33]   In any case, I find no hint whatever of any direct disagreement, or friction, or jealousy between these two ardent workers. They held meetings together occasionally till the end and after Moody's death Sankey spoke of him with the warmest affection and admiration. He repeatedly referred to their laboring together for nearly thirty years, and in the tenderest and most earnest words he repudiated any suggestion that they had ever separated to any degree whatever: "It is said we parted; but, no, we never parted until death parted us at Northfield." [34]

V

It is one of the signs of Moody's genius for adapting all sorts of means to his ends that he made such mighty use of music, for he personally had little feeling for it. It is true that he sometimes insisted, with a touch of humor, that he had music in his heart, and declared that he expected to join in the celestial choruses with all his natural vigor and enthusiasm. "Well, I don't understand music, but I can sing as well as Mr. Sankey can. I can sing from my heart." [35]   And more elaborately: "I cannot sing. I could not start 'Rock of Ages,' but I suppose I have heard it once a day for six years. I cannot sing with my lips. I cannot get it out of these thick lips of mine, but way down in my heart I sing just as well as Mr. Sankey, and it is just as acceptable to God. But when we all get to heaven, I expect to sing with Moses and the Lamb." [36] But his own admission that music in itself meant little or nothing to him is amply confirmed by those who knew him best: "He had absolutely no knowledge of music and could not even sing a note. Just what pleasure singing gave him personally is an unsolved problem, and insoluble. It has sometimes seemed to those who observed him carefully that his pleasure was an indirect one, and came from seeing its influence upon others." [37] And his son says of him: "Mr. Moody frequently showed his high appreciation of music, especially vocal music, and the prominence given to praise in all his services was an evidence of this. Few people knew, however, that he had absolutely no musical ear, being unable to distinguish one tune from another. Paradoxical as it may appear, no one more readily detected any difficulty in the singing or appreciated more highly a well-trained chorus." [38]

In other words, though his esthetic appreciation was imperfect, his psychological appreciation was keen and constant, and no man ever knew better the value of music for religious excitement and stimulation, or applied it with more intelligent care. Of course this stimulant of song, even with rhythmic motion, has been a feature of revival activity in all ages. The old Testament understood it as well as the New. It is habitual in all the religions of the East. Of the Buddhist use of it is written: "It was a frequent thing during this enthusiastic singing in chorus, for the singers to exhibit many external signs of deep emotion. Some would swoon away in rapture and roll on the ground; others would embrace one another and laugh and cry alternately. . . . As the tide of feeling rose higher, the singers, in the contagion of their joy and rapture, would imagine that Krishna himself was with them and all would become 'immersed in a sea of divine *bhakti.*' " [39] Even the American Indians are agitated by a similar rapture: "The Navajo feel that only through the ecstasy of singing can contact with the holy ones be gained for any desired end. . . . The effect of one of their long ceremonies is that of a slow rise, day by day, and hour by hour, to a tremendous crisis in which, all night, the air is shattered by continuous long singing." [40]   In Christian revivals, the Wesleys, who were skillful musicians and composers, perhaps made the most effective employment of the art.   Wesley's remark, that he "did not want the devil to have all the good tunes," is classic.   His advice to his followers as to the employment of music shows how much attention he gave to the matter: "Suit the tune to the words.   Avoid complex tunes, which it is scarcely possible to sing with devotion. . . . Do not suffer the people to sing too slow. . . . In every society let them learn to sing; and let them always learn our own tunes first." [41]

Unmusical as he was, Moody had reflected on the subject perhaps as carefully as Wesley, and while he never proposed to let the singing get away from him or become the chief feature, he set himself to get out of it every ounce of possible power and glory.   If an audience was dull and sleepy, music would arouse it and make it attentive.   If an audience was tumultuous and unruly, music would quiet it and make it attentive.   He studied the tunes not for their musical value, but for their practical use to him.   He had always an eye out for new tunes, for their rhythm, for their swing, for their significance, and when the tunes were growing a trifle threadbare, he would discard them for the time and turn to others. Again, he wholly and entirely reprobated the commercial side of music. An organist might be a great artist, a choir might be highly trained and skillful. If they were not convinced and earnest Christians, he wanted nothing to do with them. "The world has come into the church like a flood, and how often you find an ungodly choir employed to do the singing for the whole congregation; the idea that we need an ungodly man to sing praises to God! It was not long ago I heard of a church where they had an unconverted choir, and the minister saw something about the choir he didn't like, and he spoke to the chorister, but the chorister replied: 'You attend to your end of the church, and I will attend to mine.' You cannot expect the Spirit of God to work in a church in such a state as that." [42]

As in everything else, Moody was extraordinarily quick with music to take advantage of every accident of time, place, or circumstance which would heighten and intensify the effect. He himself was always emphasizing the possibilities in this direction: "Give out 'Rock of Ages, Cleft for Me,' and it won't be long before the hats will be coming off, and they will remember how their mothers sung that to them once when they were in bed, and the tears will begin to run down their cheeks, and it won't be long before they will want you to read a few verses out of the Bible, and then they will ask you to pray with them, and you will be having a prayer meeting there before you know it." [43] Or he tells the story of the hymn, "Oh, come to me," which got hold of a hardened sinner, worked into his brain or his heart, haunted him day and night, "Oh, come to me," "Oh, come to me," and at last he came. And you ought to have heard Moody tell it. [44] Or there is the incident which captured Dr. Grenfell, when he had strolled into a meeting, to hear what the evangelist had to say. A long-winded old parson was stringing together the usual petitions, when Moody, who never loved long prayers and never made them, got impatient: "While Brother Jones is finishing his prayer, let us all join in singing." And Grenfell said, "Something here worth a man's attention."

Also, Moody made his people sing, even if he couldn't sing himself. He didn't merely ask them to sing; he didn't sit by and listen. They were there to do their part and he saw that they did it. One day he had an audience of nine thousand and set them to the ringing splendor of "Joy to the World." But at first they did not get hold of it. He had one gallery sing it, then another. Then he had the women sing, then the men. Finally he let the whole, vast, mad throng take it up, and "probably never before have nine thousand men and women sung under one roof with such unison and such enthusiasm." [45] One admirable passage sums up his skill, his efforts, and his results: "He would have nothing whatever to do with a piece of music which only appealed to the sense of beauty. He could form no judgment of its value by hearing it played or sung in private. He must see it tried in a crowd, and could discover in an instant its adaptation to awaken the feelings which he needed to have in action. If it had the right ring he used it for all it was worth. 'Let the people sing,' he would shout—'let *all* the people sing. Sing that verse again. There's an old man over there who is not singing at all, let *him* sing.' No matter how long it took, he would keep the people at work until they were fused and melted." [46]

MOODY AND SANKEY

VI

Sankey's voice, considered abstractly as a mere musical instrument, does not appear to have been anything phenomenal. Satirical critics even sometimes spoke of it with severity: "When I see humanity, Boston humanity—most musical of all humanity—sit and be tortured with this astounding discord, I do not doubt humanity's devotion to the gospel." [47] A more discerning and sympathetic observer, who recognized the power and the effect, also expresses the indisputable limitations: "A very erroneous opinion seems to exist among some people that this gentleman is an accomplished singer. Nothing can be further from the truth. Mr. Sankey has no pretensions of the kind and we question if he could vocalize properly the simplest exercise in the instruction book. He has possibly never had a singing lesson in his life. His voice is a powerful baritone of small compass. He touches E flat with considerable difficulty and even E strains his voice. He sings from the chest register and his intonation is far from perfect." [48]

But this same observer goes on to point out that the force of Sankey's performance did not lie in mere technical skill, but in other characteristics so remarkable that "in many respects professional singers might take a lesson from him." To begin with, he himself felt profoundly what he sang. He prepared himself with prayer and his sensitive and nervous temperament responded to the spirit of the hymn and the stimulus of the surroundings often to the point of tears. As one observer vividly puts it: "Mr. Sankey sings with the conviction that Souls are receiving Jesus between one note and the next." [49] Also, as he felt the music, he was determined to make the people feel it. The first means for doing this was to sing so as to be understood, and it was his constant care to bring out the words with the utmost distinctness and intelligibility. The music was not the first thing, nor the only thing. Words and music must be involved together in an inextricable and impressive harmony. "Singing the Gospel" was his favorite expression. For mere purposes of praise it was not perhaps necessary that the people should understand, provided they heard. But to convince, as well as move, every word of the hymns had to carry its full meaning to every member of those vast audiences. He made the words do it. It was for this purpose that he required and contrived and obtained absolute sym-

1. NORTH FARM-HOUSE WHERE MOODY BEGAN HIS MOUNT HERMON SCHOOL. 2 STONE HALL, NORTHFIELD, MASS.

COLLEGE STUDENTS CONFERENCE.

A CORNER IN THE COLLEGE CAMP.

Mr. Moody Preaching on "the Hill Called Calvary," Outside Jerusalem.

Mr. Moody stands at direct angle of the two stars

pathetic silence, for this purpose that he rejected great organs and obstrusive accompaniments, and contented himself simply with the small reed instrument to carry the tune. His Scotch hearers objected at first to his "kistful o' whistles"; but he knew its value, and he stuck to it.

And there was far more in his method than the mere enunciation of words. Moody himself did not better understand the right moment, did not better appreciate just what tune would be effective in particular circumstances than Sankey did. If he wanted to arouse and stimulate, to inspire ardor and courage, he would sing "Hold the Fort." If he wanted to bring tears and tender emotions, he would turn to "The Ninety and Nine" or to "Watching and Waiting." As one writer expresses it, "He usually selects hymns for the opening praise with a light, joyous melody, which soon brings all hearts into sympathy, so that, as the services proceed, the majestic movement and grand harmonies of familiar long-meter hymns do not roll ineffectively around souls still insensible from worldly influence." [50] The most intense effects of dramatic management and climax were at the disposal of this instinctive artist, but he did not use them in cold blood, but gave them their full power because he himself was passionately in sympathy with their impulse.

And there is no doubt but that he touched and conquered his audiences everywhere. A. C. Benson, whom I have before quoted in a critical connection, and who was keenly alive to the weak points, as shown in the first touches of the following passage, succumbed completely to the charm: Sankey "took his place at a small harmonium, placed so near to the front of the platform that it looked as if both player and instrument must inevitably topple over; it was inexpressibly ludicrous to behold. Rolling his eyes in an affected manner, he touched a few simple chords, and then a marvelous transformation came over the room. In a sweet, powerful voice, with an exquisite simplicity combined with irresistible emotion, he sang, 'There were Ninety and Nine!' The man was transfigured. A deathly hush came over the room, and I felt my eyes fill with tears." [51] Mrs. Barbour says of the singing of the same hymn: "When you hear 'The Ninety and Nine' sung, you know of a truth that down in this corner, up in that gallery, behind that pillar which hides the singer's face from the listener, the hand of Jesus has been finding this and that and yonder lost one to place them in his fold." [52]

MOODY AND SANKEY

It would be easy to multiply instances of the effect of these penetrating and soul-stirring melodies, so sung, upon temperaments naturally susceptible to them. Sankey himself relates many such instances, in his interesting commentary upon the Gospel Songs [53] and elsewhere, and his biographers abound with more. The effect may not have been always very permanent, but sometimes it was, and it was intense while it lasted. Young, careless, dissipated hearts were sobered and purified. Old, dry, worn, and withered hearts were warmed and cheered. The cynical and the indifferent may sneer, but it means something in a man's life to have accomplished such transformations as the following passage indicates, and Sankey accomplished scores of them: " 'I was in great darkness and trouble for some days,' said a poor woman, rejoicing and yet weeping; 'and just a little time ago when Mr. Sankey was singing these words (pointing to them with her finger) "And Jesus bids me come," my bonds were broken in a moment and now I am safe in his arms.' " [54]

What interests the psychological observer in all this, as with Moody, is the effect of it upon the singer himself. Here was a man born in comparative obscurity, who passed his early years in the weary drudgery of a small government office.

Suddenly he finds himself swept into one of the most conspicuous positions of the world. Distinguished ministers recognize him and turn to him. Men and women of rank and wealth salute him humbly, and attribute to his agency the greatest comfort and contentment of their lives. The papers feature him. Crowds throng about him, wherever he goes, with eager adulation, or with noisy mockery almost as stimulating and delightful. He is a great man and knows he is, cannot help knowing. No triumphant actor, or opera-tenor, or public orator, ever had more enthusiastic audiences or more praise and flattery. What did it do to him and how did he take it? Was he eager, anxious, sensitive to admiration, sensitive to criticism? Did the comparative falling off of his later years distress him, or was the shadow of past glory enough for any man to live on? There is no light as to all this, even less than with Moody, because there is no obvious or obtainable self-analysis in the man whatever. Even the formula of such analysis as I have suggested above would have been rejected with indignation. All thought of worldly glory and success was assumed to be indifferent and forgotten. These men were about their Master's service, and personal considerations dropped completely out of sight. And so we hear over and over again that they had no thought of self, and were only anxious to do something for the glory of the Lord. It may be so. Very likely they believed it was entirely so. All I can say is, if it was entirely so, they were different from all the men I have been familiar with and profoundly different from me.

VII

As one thinks to-day of Sankey's music and his methods, of his power of reaching vast audiences and singing at them as well as to them, one dwells upon the process of manifolding which he could have accomplished by the aid of wireless, and the topic suggests some reflections upon music as the characteristic art of the modern world and especially of democracy. Though music in some form dates from the earliest spiritual development of mankind, people do not often appreciate how enormously it has evolved within the last two hundred years and with what rapidity as compared with all the other arts. The growth of mechanical invention has facilitated the development of all sorts of instrumental music; but far more than this is the evolution of music itself from the pure harmonic and melodic treatment of Bach and Händel to the subtle spiritual suggestion and interpretation of Wagner, of Richard Strauss, of the more recent Frenchmen and Russians. How this process of evolution can continue is as difficult to predict as how it can stop.

But for the people, for the mass of mankind, there is an essential quality in music which makes it peculiarly significant as a democratic art. I have already pointed out in chapter one that the varied accumulation of possible knowledge makes our enlightened era distinctively an age of ignorance. Now music is above all the art of ignorance. The great productions of literature, even in a less degree the plastic arts, require for the full enjoyment of them some background of knowledge of past history in general, of the history of art, of the subtleties and complications of the human spirit. Music appeals primarily to the emotions and sensibilities and requires only a certain aptitude of temperament in regard to these. I am not of course speaking of musical composition, which demands special training and experience of a high and difficult order. Yet all who are at all conversant with musical people must realize how peculiarly they move in a remote world of their own, in which the larger experiences and interests of human life count for less than with ordinary mortals. And it is safe to say that the average person, to be thrilled, absorbed, carried away by musical excitement, requires no education, no broader knowledge, no intellectual equipment of any kind. It is for this reason that millions can listen for hours to their radios or victrolas when they would make no response whatever to the reading of a play of Shakespeare or the sight of a picture of Titian. It is this singular correspondence to the intellectual obfuscation of the world, that makes music the art of democracy and gives it the best chance of being the art of the future.

The limit lies in the fact that so many persons are physiologically or psychologically incapable of responding to musical stimuli at all. We have seen that Moody did not know one tune from another and did not care for any. Millions, especially men, are like Moody in this respect. Either their hearing, otherwise keen and sensitive enough, remains insusceptible to the contrasts and differentiations of melody and harmony; or the intense excitement of rhythmic progression is completely lost upon them; or their processes of association and suggestion are untouched by the thrills and throbs which stir others almost to madness. And this limitation is in no way confined to the ignorant or the primitive. Some of the most intensely esthetic temperaments in the world are destitute of musical ardor. Indeed, it sometimes seems as if great writers, so peculiarly sensitive to the rhythmic and melodic charm of words, were more indifferent or even hostile than other people to the distinctive and compelling rapture of music. So it seems likely that mankind will always be divided into those for whom music may open the deepest secrets of the soul and those to whom it opens nothing whatever.

But there can be no question as to the enormous influence of music for people, and they are perhaps a majority, who really feel its power. The very vagueness, the very absence of dry, intellectual, logical requirement, the immediate, intense appeal to association and emotion, tease us out of thought, involve us, dissolve us in a region of vast, unsatisfied desire, of eternal, tantalizing, transfiguring question, of inexplicable hope. Emerson, who was himself quite indifferent to music, was at least able to seize this quality in it:

> "And music pours on mortals
> Its beautiful disdain." [55]

And he quotes the passionate exclamation of Richter in regard to it: "Away! Away! thou speakest to me of things which in all my endless life I have not found and shall not find." [56]

It is unnecessary to point out that these fundamental musical emotions are not essentially or exclusively religious. A large part of them are not religious at all; but on the contrary, as I have made plain at the beginning of this chapter, they tend constantly to sweep us into regions altogether alien to the religious life. Long ago the Greeks, so sensitive to spiritual distinctions and so quick to analyze them, recognized that certain forms of music were antipathetic to serious and elevated thought and even to elementary morality and did their best to discourage or prohibit them. How intense and earnest Christian feeling must view the matter is well indicated in a very remarkable passage from the letters of William Cowper, though to most average people, even Christians, Cowper's attitude will seem extreme, if not abnormal: "The lawfulness of music, when used in moderation and in its proper place, is unquestionable; but I believe that wine itself, though a man be guilty of habitual intoxication, does not more debauch and befool the natural understanding than music,—always music, music in season and out of season,—weakens and destroys the spiritual discernment. If it is not used with an unfeigned reference to the worship of God, and with a design to assist the soul in the performance of it, which cannot be the case when it is the only occupation, it degenerates into a sensual delight and becomes a most powerful advocate for the admission of other pleasures, grosser perhaps in degree, but in their kind the same." [57] This is being a little severe on the thousands who pass evening after evening with the apparently mild and harmless delights of the radio. But those who look a little more subtly into the wild exhilaration of the dance, the dissipating, dissolving suggestion of passionate popular song, even the questioning, despairing, insatiable moods that come with much great orchestral and vocal music, will have no difficulty in understanding what Cowper means. I have already quoted the song of Feste in "Twelfth Night,"

"What is love? 'Tis not hereafter."
If we are to let our ideal Shakespearean clown run through all these varying chapters as the counter-type of everything that Moody stands for in

the world, surely there is nothing like the ecstasy of the love-song and the mad rapture that goes with it to embody the grace and the charm and the enthralling magic and the wickedness of the primrose way that leads to the everlasting bonfire.

And then there is the music that leads the other way, to heaven. No one can deny the rapture and the absorbing, fulfilling ecstasy of that. What it must be for the believer, the regenerate, the sanctified, naturally no one but the sanctified can wholly convey, as not even the sanctified can explain it. But perhaps the record of one of the profane, who has found in religious music some of the intensest, though certainly not the happiest experiences of life, may have a certain interest for those who have gone through the same and even for those who have not. From my earliest childhood I was accustomed to having the family gather about the piano on Sunday evenings and sing hymns of all sorts. No words of mine can express the misery that those hymns caused me. The nature of it I cannot analyze and the cause of it I cannot explain. It may have been that I had a sense that I should be a Christian and was not, but I do not think it had any such definite origin as that and I imagine it went far deeper. Never,

never will there pass from my soul the memory of youthful prayer-meetings in a little dreary church vestry. The place was dreary, the people were dreary, the prayers and the discourses were ineffably dreary. And then, to the harsh accompaniment of the little reed organ, would come the swell of voices carrying on those indescribable, incomparable hymns, and my heart would overflow with an unearthly blending of rapture and question and despair. For years, indeed for nearly all my life, the impression persisted in just this form, and the distress associated with them made me fly like the plague the singing of hymns in any shape. Oddly enough, with the approach of age, with the depressing, withering blight of illness settling down upon me, with the deadly imminence of the grave, my feeling has changed and of late I have been imploring my wife to sing to me the very hymns that up to five years ago I could not endure. And again the feeling that comes with them is so complicated and entangled that I cannot analyze it. There is as much of grief and despair in it as of ecstasy. But what I once detested now becomes comforting with a tortured mixture of desire and delight.

If others have not felt something of what I have

described above, my words are wasted. But if, as I feel sure, they have, it simply shows the immense, inestimable power which music has, or may have, to overcome men's souls.

VIII

And there is no question but that Moody and Sankey handled this powerful and subtle spiritual agency with extraordinary skill. They might not have affected the audience of a symphony concert, and again they might. They certainly produced a prodigious effect upon the audiences with which they had to deal, and exactly the effect they wished to produce. This effect in general is well described by the critic of a London musical paper, who was not especially in sympathy with the religious effort of the evangelists, but who appreciated perfectly when people were being carried away: "Even the critical musician will allow its prodigious grandeur—a grandeur far different from that of a Händel Festival, but more impressive, as it is natural, spontaneous, and enthusiastic. No puerility in the words, no consecutive fifths or solecisms in the music, affects those who sing; and the infantile tune becomes magnificent in the surge of ten thousand voices." [58] And the power of Sankey's hymns extended far beyond even the limits of the monster meetings. There is the old saying: "Let me make the songs of a country, and I care not who makes the laws." The hymns got out into the streets and were sung and whistled and murmured by thousands who did not know or care where they came from, but who felt their power all the same. When you think how many million lips "Sweet By and By" and "Watching and Waiting" have passed over, surely their significance is enormously increased for any one.

In the various, vague, baffling, confused, unsatisfying portrayals of heaven it is interesting to see how constantly music bears a conspicuous part, and on the whole this is explicable enough. Certainly one can not picture heaven as a revival meeting, with Moody's God the central figure on the platform, flanked by a beatific assemblage of the clergy, the very sight of whom would elicit groans from the profane, who, to be sure, are not expected to be present. Nor would a symphony concert altogether answer. It suggests too many women who come to see and to be seen and to wear apparel which is in no way appropriate to celestial surroundings. But perhaps the most adequate conception, where all are forlornly inadequate, is that of the eternity of one rapturous instant, such as in this world are too transitory almost to be registered and too exhausting for mortal endurance. The Mohammedans are supposed to have asserted such a conception in its grossest form. But of the finer spiritual raptures, which envelop and enthrall us with an unutterable transport of oblivion, none surely are more intense for those who are susceptible of them, as none are more wayward, more elusive, more intangible, than the rapture music brings. The supreme moment may come with the performance of a Beethoven symphony. It may come with one's own solitary, imperfect rendering of a prelude of Bach or a waltz of Chopin. It may come with the singing of a bird in a spring morning or a summer twilight. It may come when a thousand voices are ringing out the chorus of a Gospel Hymn. It comes and goes in this world with celestial evanescence. But when it comes, it brings heaven with it, and rendered permanent in its supreme intensity, it becomes a type of heaven not wholly unworthy.

CHAPTER V

MOODY THE MAN

I

HENRY DRUMMOND is said to have remarked that Moody was "the greatest human he had ever met." It is impossible to live long with Moody and not realize what Drummond meant. The evangelist may have had the fundamentals of saintliness, he may have lived intimately with the thought of the other world, but he was also splendidly constituted to exist in this. He was human not only by the ample solid vigor of his bodily frame, but by his large interest in men, women, and children, his quick insight into their motives, passions, and characters, his tender and sympathetic soul.

It appears that, until towards the end, when his heart began to fail him, Moody had constant, magnificent health. The robust material frame, sustained by clean and temperate living, was always equal to any strain he might choose to put upon it. In a sense he took good care of himself, but he did not need to take the care that most men do. He wanted little sleep, and that little he could take anywhere at any time. His rare references to ill health only prove what an insignificant thing it was in his life. When he was in Chicago, he tells us, he saw an advertisement of "Pain-Killer." He did not pay much attention. He had no pain and needed nothing to kill it. "But one morning when spring came, I had a headache, and when I saw that this Pain-Killer would cure headache, I bought a bottle."[1] He had to buy precious few bottles of that kind. His health was not only sufficient, it was exuberant, the kind that of itself breeds hope and confidence and joy. There was in him a riotous abundance of life, such as forms the securest basis of optimism. It is chiefly to vigor like his that Emerson's sentence applies: "Give me health and a day and I will make the pomp of emperors ridiculous."

And his health was at the bottom of that unfailing activity and rush which were the admiration and the despair of all Moody's fellow-workers. He could not only set a dozen men at work, but he could outwork them. Here again there are occasional references to fatigue which serve only to show how tremendous the energy was. When he had engaged to speak to a vast audience at Aberdeen, he suddenly found that his voice had almost gone with a cold. But he began to speak just the same and spoke and spoke, till he had worked the hoarseness all out of it. As one observer expressed it: "When a man gets a bad cold, and goes on with such colossal work without intermission, one comes to ask, 'Is he made of iron only in figure, or is he really so?' " [2] In one instance, after incredible exertion, Moody himself gave up, and said to his associate, "It is no use: I am too tired. You must take the service." The friend assented. But when the hour came, there was Moody, and he took charge of the meeting with more effect than usual.[3]

The magnificent vitality persisted till death. Indeed, one cannot help feeling that it was the vitality more than anything that seemed to sweep Moody right on into another world. Doubts about a future life belong to the pale, the anemic, the discouraged, in this. He could not die: there was no die to him. There is something triumphant, exultant, about the whole description of his departure. When he was at death's door, he suddenly seemed to revive: "I'm going to get up. If God wants to heal me by a miracle that way, all right; and if not, I can meet death in my chair as well as here." [4] When he did go, it was with a calm, assured confidence that it was only to a change, and to a glorious change.

His solid frame, running in his later years to over two hundred and fifty pounds, of course required large and substantial nourishment. In this respect he was like Phillips Brooks, who is said to have shunned private tables and preferred a hotel where he could eat all he wanted. Moody's superb digestion scorned ordinary rules. He ate what he pleased when he pleased and apparently never suffered for it. Dr. Goss gives a vivid, sympathetic description of the process: "Dashing into my house one evening after a day of terrific effort, he exclaimed, 'Have you got anything to eat?' A large dish of pork and beans (of which he was very fond) was placed before him. He sat down, murmured a silent prayer, and, without interrupting his repast by a word, emptied the entire dish as fast as he could carry the food to his mouth. And yet this was done with a certain indefinable grace. He often ate voraciously, but never like an animal nor ever like an epicure."[5] His drink was proportioned to his eating; but it is doubtful whether he ever even tasted alcohol, unless for some medicinal purpose.

Moody was as human in all his relations with

his fellows as in his person. He was adored by his family and thoroughly deserved it. He was a great lover of home, and perhaps the love was not diminished by very frequent absence. I wish there was some suggestion of early affairs of the heart. With so warm and impulsive a temperament one feels that there must have been such; but there is only the vaguest trace of them, and no allusion anywhere in Moody's own writing to indicate anything of the kind. He is said to have been very reticent about his own concerns,[6] and on this point he certainly was so. Even of the love-affair which led to his marriage and which one would imagine must have been charming there is no account whatever, nothing at all resembling the delightful narrative of General Booth's wooing of his Catharine.

Yet it is certain that the love was most satisfactory in its results. Mrs. Moody seems to have been just the woman for an evangelist's wife. Her path cannot always have been smooth. To be sure, she had few difficulties of temper to contend with. Her husband speaks of having had a temper in his youth and one can easily imagine some manifestations of it. But the universal testimony is that in his home he was sunny and sweet. On the other

Mr. and Mrs. Moody with Grandchildren.

MARQUAND HALL, NORTHFIELD SEMINARY.

NORTHFIELD SEMINARY BUILDINGS AND CAMPUS FROM THE EAST.

THE CONNECTICUT RIVER, WITH NORTHFIELD SEMINARY IN THE DISTANCE.
Showing road to South Vernon.

hand, he was unexpected, always surging in and sweeping out, bringing the most astonishing things and people in his train. But apparently he could not disconcert Mrs. Moody. She took the unexpectedness with admirable adaptability and calm. Moody's own references to her are always charming, and he brings her into his sermons with a sweet natural reminiscence: "My wife, I think, would think it a very strange feeling if I should tell how I loved her the first year we were married and how happy I was then. It would break her heart." [7] Again: "If my wife were in a foreign country, and I had a beautiful mansion all ready for her, she would a good deal rather I should come and take her unto it than to have me send some one else to bring her." [8] His trust in her, his dependence upon her, seem to have been unlimited. He felt that she could do even his own work better than he: "When I have an especially hard case, I turn him over to my wife; she can bring a man to a decision for Christ where I cannot touch him." [9] And her place and value in the household are well indicated in the remark of her son Paul: "My mother was the buffer between himself and the world. She was the 'shockabsorber.' She stood between him and things." [10]

D. L. MOODY: A WORKER IN SOULS

Nothing is more attractive about Moody personally than his relations with his children. He was a great lover of children in general, liked to play with them and tease them and comfort them and watch them. When people objected to babies in church, he said let them come. It is better that the mother should be in church with the baby than stay at home to take care of it. His sermons are full of stories about children and of illustrations drawn from them, and he was interested not only in their religious welfare but in their having a good time right here in this world.

When it came to his own children, he was inexhaustible in interest, attention, and ingenuity. Here again was material for his sermons, and the boys and girls are constantly introduced, not tediously, he was far too wise for that, but with apt and pointed suggestion. He uses their child hopes and child tears, their wayward fancies and petulant insistence, their dependence, their pitifulness, their affection. It is evident that his methods of discipline were steady, thoughtful, severe when necessary, but always intelligent and directed rather to permanent improvement than to immediate convenience. Take the story of his little daughter Emma and her own willful choice of the doll. "One day," he says, "I had a good streak come over me and I took her to a toy shop to get her a doll." Emma's fancy was taken by a cheap affair near the door and, after protesting, her father bought it for her for a nickel. The doll was soon forgotten, and when the father pointed out that he meant to buy a big one that would have been more costly, the child said, "Why didn't you?" "Because you wouldn't let me. You remember you wanted that little doll and you would have it." "The little thing saw the point and she bit her lips and did not say any more. From that day to this I cannot get her to say what she wants. When I was going to Europe the last time I asked her what she wanted me to bring her, and she said, 'Anything you like!'" And then the moral: "It is far better to let God choose for us than to choose for ourselves." [11] Thus the family affections, like everything else, served to forward the work of God.

Like all parents, but perhaps more intelligently than most, he looked forward to the future of his children, made plans for them and tried to shape their lives in the way that would be most profitable for themselves and for the world. He considered not only their religious welfare, but was

anxious that they should have the best possible
education, with the view that it would make them
both happier and more serviceable. But the service was the thing that he chiefly thought of, and
in nobly defining his own aim in life he clearly
outlined his conception of theirs: "I have always
been an ambitious man, ambitious to leave no
wealth or possessions, but to leave lots of work for
you to do." [12]

Independent of all ambition or aspiration, however, he simply enjoyed his children, and it seems
that few parents could enjoy them more. How
delightful is this glimpse creeping right into the
midst of a formal talk: "I remember once I was
very busy getting up a sermon, and my little boy
came into the room. I wanted to get rid of him
just as quickly as possible. And I said to him,
'My son, what do you want?' He threw his arms
around my neck and kissed me and said, 'I don't
want anything, I just love you.' I couldn't send
him away, and I got down all his toys for him and
let him stay in the room with me; and every once
in a while I looked over my book and seen him
just as happy as he could be." [13] He would romp
with the children, enter wildly into their plays,
and if a solemn and distinguished stranger entered,

he was invited to join, and the romp grew only wilder. Then in a moment some scriptural suggestion would enter the father's head. He would reach for the Bible and the whole family was turned with due decorum into a Bible class, but I am inclined to think he felt in his heart that God would have enjoyed the romping too. And under the playful affection and tenderness the deeper thought was always hidden. These young lives were confided to his care, and he was going to keep them turned heavenward, if he could: "I have two sons, and no one but God knows how I love them; but I would see their eyes dug out of their heads rather than see them grow up to manhood and go down to the grave without Christ and without hope." [14] His grandchildren were almost dearer to him than his children and the deaths among them wrung his heart.

To bring up and educate three children and to maintain a moderate but most comfortable home and establishment it is evident that money was needed in pretty constant supply, and the nature of this supply in Moody's case is rather obscure. He had a natural aptitude for business, when he left it he had already amassed a tidy sum, and would no doubt soon have made a fortune. But when he gave himself up to religious work, he threw this world's fortune all aside and placed his dependence entirely upon the Lord. It appears that from that time to the end he was supported by voluntary contributions of one sort or another from his friends and admirers. Sometimes there must have been very tight pinches. Sometimes when the supply was scanty the only resort seemed to be to prayer, and prayer was almost always found effective. One thing that must above all be emphasized was that in this matter of money, as in everything else, Moody's sincerity and honesty were above question and above reproach. As we have seen, he utterly renounced the profit from the Gospel Hymns and persuaded Sankey to do the same. "He told me during the World's Fair," says Dr. Torrey, "that if he had taken, for himself, the royalties on the hymn books which he had published they would have amounted, at that time, to a million dollars." [15] Even as to direct gifts, he was often hesitating and inclined to refuse them, saying that he could get along without. "Millions of dollars passed into Mr. Moody's hands," says Dr. Torrey again, *but they passed through;* they did not stick to *his* fingers." [16] Nothing hurt him more than the suggestion, too often made, that he

was using his great ministry for private profit, and
no suggestion certainly could have been more un-
just. His innumerable wealthy friends would
have been glad to do far more for him than they
did. But he asked only security for himself and
his family, so that his hands might be free.

The result seems to have been a rather queerly
mixed economic establishment, and there must
have been some problems distinctly perplexing to
a good housewife. The husband was a splendid
financier on the larger scale, but he was too absorbed for details. One morning in the early days
the wife asked him to send up a barrel of flour.
In the evening she thanked him for its arrival.
"Flour?" said he. "I ordered no flour, forgot all
about it." [17] He had not provided, but the Lord
had. Nevertheless, the Lord's provision was
pretty constantly generous. When one thinks of
Moody's start in the world and of the prospects
of the petty shoe-clerk, one is rather overcome with
the prosperity and comfort of his later years.
When he traveled, he stayed in luxurious hotels,
or in still more luxurious private houses. When
he was at home, his house, if not luxurious, had
certainly every accommodation that the most exact-
ing could require. Nobody could say that in his

case the service of the Lord involved any very irksome sacrifice. Yet at the same time the money went as it came, and when he died he told his children that he had not a penny to leave them, except their immortal hope and an infinite possibility of service.

Moody not only had a comfortable home, but a farm at Northfield, and got infinite amusement out of it, indeed more amusement than profit. He was a practical farmer both from boyhood experience and from wide observation. No doubt he would have been quite capable of the remark of old Dr. Ripley, when asked to pray for a certain field: "This field don't need prayer, it needs manure." When he was abroad, he liked to pick up rare and valuable seeds for home experimentation.[18] He liked to raise poultry and to watch them. Above all, he had the proverbial minister's fancy for good horseflesh. Scandalous and wholly unfounded stories were told of the prices he paid for thoroughbred horses. But he liked a horse that would go and was willing to pay for him.

Such a domestic establishment, however simple, evidently required servants, both indoors and out. I do not find much light on Moody's relations with these; but what there is, together with the character of the man, makes it clear that he treated them as human helpers and not in any way as inferiors. There is the pretty story of the man who was working in the fields on a hot day, as his employer drove by. "Bigelow," said Moody, "it's too hot for you to work much; half a day's work for a day's pay, you know, while this heat lasts." [19] That was the spirit. Or as he put it more generally: "A good many have trouble with servants. Did you ever think that the trouble lies with you instead of the servants?" [20]

The truth was, he felt that he was a servant, servant of men, servant of God. Life took its true significance from service, and the only thing that could possibly make service degrading was to be ill done. Moreover, he was apter to serve himself in everything than any one else could be. What is most notable about him in these domestic and in all practical matters is his quickness in doing the proper, suitable, important thing, and doing it right. He had the Yankee skill with his hands. He had more than the Yankee instinct for meeting all sorts of situations, for seizing the appropriate and perhaps even more for shunning the inappropriate. In the mad confusion of the Chicago fire, when all his household goods were perishing, his wife, usually a practical woman enough, put into his hands to carry away the oil painting of himself, which she above all wanted to save. He laughed at her: "How would I look carrying a picture of myself through the Chicago streets?" Just so he met all the problems of life and solved them or avoided them deftly, with that supreme gift of tact which most ensures success and which is most envied by those who hesitate and stumble and blunder and think of the right word and deed only when it is too late.

II

The ample humanity of Moody was equally interesting and engaging when he crossed his own threshold and entered into the larger social relations of the world. Few men have met a greater number of their fellows than he. He saw all sorts of people in all sorts of places, and he was cordial and friendly with them all, and treated each after his own fashion and in his own spirit. He remembered names and faces with astonishing accuracy, considering the multitudes with whom he came into contact. I doubt whether he had very intimate friends, to whom he opened himself with entire unreserve. There is no sign of such friends holding over from boyhood, and they rarely appear in a man's later life. Too vast general acquaintance is hardly favorable to the development of them. But it is obvious that Moody was singularly beloved by many people. The delicate sensibility and high intelligence of a Henry Drummond responded to his winning qualities just as readily as the simpler heart of a laborer about his Northfield home. One of the teachers in the Mount Hermon school, who had known him intimately and loved him, counted it among the promises of heaven, as she lay upon her deathbed, that she should see Mr. Moody. And in the same way his own warm heart poured forth an infinite tenderness over those to whom he had become attached. When Drummond's death was announced to him, "that evening at my table," says Dr. Goss, "he laid his knife and fork down and cried like a child: 'He was the most Christlike man I ever met, I never saw a fault in him,' he said over and over again through his sobs." [21] He is reported to have burst into tears in a public meeting over the death of the gospel-singer Bliss.

He was indeed by nature thoroughly social, and liked to have people about him, to see and talk with them and enter into their interests, and especially to save their souls. It could not be said that he was averse to solitude. He had always God with him, and the Bible, and a tumult of thoughts. Nevertheless, human faces and voices were acceptable and diverting, and he warmed to them with a singular, spontaneous tenderness, which no one could resist or fail to feel. "Tears start to the eyes of those who knew Mr. Moody well," says Dr. Goss, "at the thought of the absolutely inexhaustible depths of his love for all living things. Horses, dogs, cows, animals, and birds—all excited the emotions of his heart. In the realm of human life, love for all classes was a master passion." [22] The love was indeed perfectly democratic and knew no difference between rich and poor, gentle and simple. The common human touch was all that was needed. Moody lived a good deal with the wealthy, in England he lived with rank and titles. But these things meant nothing to him. One evening at a great meeting in London, a certain peer was introduced. "Glad to meet you, Lord. Just get two chairs for those old ladies over there, will you?" That was the spirit. You might be an emperor, you might be a clown. You had a soul to save, and in any case it was worth saving. Beyond that it was all one to Moody.

And as he met people easily in the wider world, so he was always anxious to have them come to him. His doors stood open with the freest hospitality and there was a warm welcome at all times for everybody. "No man ever surpassed Mr. Moody in hospitality. Introduce a stranger to him, and after the first salutation he would say, 'Come and dine with me,' or, if it was evening, 'Come and take supper and spend the night at my house.' His house, which was large and commodious, was usually full of guests, and his table was often crowded." [23]

Whatever guests came were sure to be amply entertained, not only materially, but intellectually and spiritually. They saw that their entertainer was heartily enjoying himself, and they also enjoyed themselves. "Who that ever sat about his table can forget his laugh? It was as hearty a laugh as one has ever heard. He knew just how to put every man at his best. His questions always brought forth that which would make a man appear to his best advantage before his hearers." [24] Could any social gifts be more attractive? Then there were the stories. Moody himself was an inexhaustible, a riotous story teller, and he had, what some story tellers have not, an almost equal delight in the stories of others. What a vivid picture does

Dr. Stebbins give of a day's entertainment in this kind: "There was one day stands out in my memory when the stories began, one following another, causing roars of laughter that continued until it seemed as if we no longer had strength to endure it. Mr. Sankey went to one side of the room and, with his head on his arms, leaned against the window, and I to another room suffering with pain, each laughing immoderately at the veritable side-splitting incidents that were related." [25] This does not exactly suggest an atmosphere of pervading Puritanic gloom.

And Moody had wit too, a surprising, unfailing aptitude for quick retort, which I have already more than once illustrated. Sometimes this manifested itself in mere badinage, the rapid thrust and exchange of the verbal duelist who darts his weapon hither and thither for the mere delight of dexterity and practice. But the wit was just as ready and effective in serious crises and served to bring out the deepest points of argument with an agility as dazzling as it was simple. When the ministers of London questioned the evangelist upon points of creed and doctrine, he answered them with a speed and spirit so noble and adequate that they could not resist him. [26] Again, when a man asked him the pointed question, "How can I get the speakers to be short in the prayer-meetings?" he replied, "Be short yourself, and set a good example." [27] A lesson that is driven home like that is not forgotten.

Moody not only liked wit, quick retorts, jolly and side-splitting stories, but, in spite of his serious and passionate pursuits, he was always more or less addicted to the practical jokes that had delighted his youth. In later years he perhaps did not carry these quite so far as in the story of the cobbler under whose leather seat the joker placed a pan of water, so that every time his victim sat down he settled into the water, while when he rose, the elastic seat sprang up and concealed the trap.[28] But as the staid father of a family he liked to come down to breakfast and after the blessing had been decorously asked, slyly squirt water with his spoon over the children assembled. We have seen that when he and Sankey were being ferried across the Connecticut River, Moody surreptitiously pulled back while the ferryman pulled forward, so as to prolong the trip. In the same way, when the Mount Hermon boys got him to take part in a tug-of-war, he managed to act as "anchor" and then to tie his end of the rope around a convenient tree, so that his opponents were trying to uproot a solid oak.

Unlike some confirmed jesters of this order, Moody was always good-naturedly ready to accept an exchange. As he himself put it, "No man has a right to play a joke unless he's willing to take one." [29] One day he leaned out of the window of his train, as it stopped at a country station, and said eagerly to a farmer who looked like a promising subject, "Do you know that President Lincoln is on this train?" The farmer bit at once, and exclaimed, "Is he?" "I don't know that he is," was the calm answer, "but I thought you might." The farmer turned away and resumed his walk on the platform. Pretty soon he came back. "We've had quite a little excitement here lately," he remarked. "What's the matter?" asked Moody. "The authorities wouldn't let some folks bury a woman," replied the farmer. "Why not?" "Because she wasn't dead," was the adequate answer.[30] And Moody enjoyed it as much as the farmer did. Also he enjoyed the comment of a caustic neighbor who assured him that there was one thing he and Sankey might do which would create a tremendous, beneficent stir, if they would only do it, but he was sure they never could. "Do

THE NORTHFIELD HOME OF MR. MOODY

MR. MOODY HAILING A FRIEND.

A snap shot.

MR. MOODY AS HIS TOWNSFOLK KNEW HIM.

tell us what it is; we want to know." "If you and Sankey would mind your own business." [31]

Obviously this is all rather crude, and for the subtler forms of humor, such as appealed to spirits like Lincoln and Charles Lamb, Moody would have had little appreciation and little liking. Humor of this kind is always closely allied to melancholy, being partly a relief from it and partly closely blended with it, and melancholy was utterly remote from Moody's solid nerves and buoyant temper. Humor of the higher intellectual type rests upon a pervading sense of the insignificance of life, not only of the life of this world, which Moody too despised, but of the life of any world, the insignificance of joy and grief alike in face of the vast blank of eternity, most of all the insignificance of self. Such humor is a universal dissolvent, dissolves life and death and even God. Moody's tremendous affirmation did not dissolve, but crystallized the swift fluidity of life around one immense, all-absorbing, endlessly active ego. And again we have the opposite type in the Shakespearean clown, embodying as we may suppose the deepest humorous instinct of Shakespeare himself.

"A foolish thing is but a toy,
 For the rain it raineth every day."

D. L. MOODY: A WORKER IN SOULS

In spite of his strong social instinct and unfailing interest in the pursuits and activities of men, Moody seems to have cared little for the ordinary diversions and amusements of life. We have seen that esthetic pleasures did not mean much to him: music, painting, poetry; perhaps these can hardly be classed as social. But there is little sign of his taking any interest in outdoor sports of any kind, unless his love for driving good horses may be called such, and I do not remember any mention of his riding, except as matter of necessity. He encouraged athletic sports at Mount Hermon School, probably because he thought they fostered some elements of manliness. But there is no record of his hunting or fishing or taking any conspicuous part in games of strength or agility, though his quickness of practical intelligence might well have enabled him to excel in them. There is, of course, no possible reason to imagine that he lacked physical courage any more than physical strength. It is indeed always something of a puzzle why he did not enlist in the Civil War, as Sankey did; but it is said, no doubt with truth, that he was extremely averse to the idea of slaughtering his fellow creatures.

At any rate, he showed himself physically brave

enough in all sorts of critical situations, and he had that most valuable element of courage, the gift of keeping your wits about you and being apt to act as well as to endure. When the big unruly boys in his classes bothered him, he usually subdued them by reason or by kindness or by prayer. But if the occasion seemed to call for it, he did not hesitate to subdue them by the plain use of his fists, and he could do it effectively. When he was exposed to peril by sea, his self-control and confidence were an example to every one. When a portion of the roof fell in at one of his great meetings, nothing but his coolness prevented a disastrous panic, and an ex-Confederate general, who knew what courage was, remarked to a bystander: "I have seen many brave men in my life put into positions of great personal danger, and I believe I know a brave man when I see him tested. I want to say to you that I have never seen a braver man than D. L. Moody." [32] But the courage and the coolness were not preferably displayed in athletic contests of physical strength.

Naturally this indifference to sports became vigorous hostility when they tended to infringe upon the Sabbath. We have seen how Moody hated Sunday papers. He was equally bitter against racing or baseball or any other outdoor contest that encroached upon the Lord's Day. Nor was he in the least disposed to be friendly to attempts to make the churches popular by associating amusement with them. Such attempts seemed to him insidious, dissipating, and in the end destructive. "Oh, I got so sick of such parties that I left years ago; I would not think of spending a night that way; it is a waste of time; there is hardly a chance to say a word for the Master. If you talk of a personal Christ, your company becomes offensive; they don't like it; they want you to talk about the world, about a popular minister, a popular church, a good organ, a good choir, and they say, 'Oh, we have a grand organ, and a superb choir,' and all that, and it suits them, but that doesn't warm the Christian heart." [33] He would have warmly endorsed the remark of William James: " 'When a church has to be run by oysters, ice-cream and fun,' I read in an American religious paper, 'you may be sure that it is running away from Christ.' Such, if one may judge by appearances, is the present plight of many of our churches." [34]

The objections on account of Sunday of course applied with as much force to indoor games and pastimes as to outdoor, and I have no evidence that Moody was more friendly to the former than to those of an athletic order. In the early enthusiasm of conversion he came one night upon a harmless game of checkers. "In an instant he seized the board, dashed it to pieces, and before a word could be spoken, dropped upon his knees and began to pray." [35] No doubt in later years he grew outwardly more tolerant; but it is by no means certain that he would not have liked to adopt the same methods to the end of his life. Cards were anathema to him, and billiards were almost identical with alcohol and tobacco, both of which he hated and pursued with the utmost virulence. When he was asked if he could cite any verse of the Bible that condemned smoking, he answered, "No, I can give you no verses in the Bible against the habit of smoking, but I can give you a verse in favor of it; 'He that is filthy, let him be filthy still.' " [36]

Dancing he does not frequently refer to, probably because he regarded it as too far outside the pale even for discussion. When a young lady suggested that it might be permissible among family friends, he said to her: "My dear girl, I would a thousand times rather have you get more grace in your heart and less in your heels." [37] The theater he introduces often, and always to condemn it. If he had known Pascal's vivid words about it, he would certainly have approved them: "All the great diversions are dangerous for Christian life; but among all those that the world has invented none is more to be feared than the theater. It represents the passions so naturally and so delightfully that it begets them in our hearts, above all that of love, and chiefly when love is represented as chaste and above reproach." [38] But he has words of his own about the theater, which, if less subtle than Pascal's, are quite as scathing: "I don't know of a theater, from Maine to California, that hasn't a bar connected with it, or near by. What is that bar there for? Fallen women go to the theaters, and for no good purpose, whenever they can. You say it is part of one's education to see good plays. Let that kind of education go to the four winds. For a child of God to help build up such an institution as the theater of the present day is iniquitous." And he adds the appalling story of a wealthy elder of the church who used to call him bigoted in his ideas on these subjects. Soon after, the said elder's son, a married man, fell in love with a wicked woman, who shot him

through the heart. "He had got acquainted with
her at the theater and she claimed him." [39] You
see how logical it is.

As regards all these matters of amusement, the
reflection that suggests itself is simply that Moody
required no diversion, no distraction, no intoxication, because he lived all the time with the greatest of intoxications, that of saving men's souls
and making their bodies do his bidding.

III

Moody's attitude towards the larger serious human interests of this world is exceedingly interesting as are also the motives for that attitude.
Wherever he came into immediate personal contact, his natural warmth and tenderness of heart
took right hold of the human side and responded
to it. It appears that in his home town of Northfield he was greatly and generally beloved. Probably there were cases of minor hostility and
grudge. If there were not, it would be very unusual, since the greater the man, the greater the
local envy as well as the local pride is apt to be.
But if there were such cases, not a trace of them
has drifted into my reading anywhere. Moody
knew the farmers and their wives, and they knew

him. They took an interest in his doings and a pride in them, even if they occasionally criticized. He is said to have been always active in movements to improve the town, and he subscribed money liberally, being among the first to respond to an appeal for the building of a Catholic Church. When the Village Improvement Society was formed, "he subscribed $100.00 to improve the street, knowing it would be expended in a part of the village remote from the school and from his residence." [40] So far as Northfield was concerned, he was certainly a public-spirited citizen, and the building and development of his educational institutions gave the town an inward activity and an external reputation which it would otherwise hardly have acquired.

In the same way his personal kindness and consideration for others were unlimited. He was always on the lookout for those smaller helpfulnesses to friends and neighbors which go so far. His mother, even in her narrow circumstances, had brought up her children to be kind to those whose circumstances were still narrower, [41] and the son never forgot the mother's lessons. It is said that he encouraged his wife and daughter to interest themselves in helping the sick and needy in all parts of the town.[42] Where money would answer he gave it readily, and where money failed, he was equally ready with advice and comfort. A pretty instance of the quick response of his energetic sympathy is told by his son. One day in later years, when Moody had settled himself for a morning's uninterrupted work, he chanced to look out of the window and saw a student evidently leaving the Conferences for the station and trudging along with an immensely heavy bag. Moody put the matter out of his head, but somehow when he tried to fix his thoughts upon the Bible, always that boy with the heavy bag kept getting in the way. Finally, he says, "I couldn't stand it any longer. I went to the barn and hurriedly had my horse hitched up, overtook the young man, and carried him and his baggage to the station. When I returned to the house I had no further difficulty in fixing my attention on the subject." [43] It is said that in the same way, partly through kindness and partly for fun, he used often to present himself at the train to meet guests, dressed in rough farmer's garb, and posing at first as a local driver with no other function.

When we go into the outside world, however, and deal with the great practical matters of life, the situation is oddly changed, and all at once Moody seems very far off. Take business. He recognizes the importance of business in the world, and heaven knows few were more expert at it than he. Yet his relation to necessary business was, perhaps not unnaturally, one of a certain amount of protest: "When a man will drive like Jehu all the week and like a snail on Sunday, isn't there something wrong with him?" [44] When it comes to politics, the remoteness is vastly accentuated. It is indeed said that in his youth, before he had settled to harness, as it were, he showed symptoms of turning his immense activity in political directions. In 1856 he was strongly in favor of abolition and took an energetic, if petty, part in the campaign for the election of Fremont. [45] In his very last years he was a hearty advocate and admirer of McKinley and was greatly concerned about the progress of the Spanish War. [46] Also, he occasionally lays some emphasis upon patriotism. He commends the prophet Daniel, because "he not only loved his God, but he loved his country. I like to see a patriotic man." [47] No doubt he himself was in the abstract honestly and earnestly patriotic and would have responded to any compelling public appeal. In general, however, it is astonishing how little public matters appear in his pages and how little record there is of his taking any active part or even any interest in them. Government questions, all the eager agitation for this and that political change or improvement,—these were not his affair. Probably he would have felt with Dr. Johnson that individual happiness or unhappiness, and still more individual sin and salvation, remained about the same under any and all governments. It does not appear that he identified himself ever very seriously with any political party. No doubt he voted dutifully, but in general he did little more. When you think of the active political part played by many prominent preachers, Theodore Parker, Phillips Brooks, Edward Hale, Henry Ward Beecher, you cannot fail to find Moody's complete abstinence and indifference somewhat curious. On the other hand, there is no doubt that his general detachment from political partisanship made his revival work more acceptable everywhere, and it is probable that, with his unfailing acuteness, he was quite well aware of this. Thus he could go into the South very soon after the Civil War and be well received.

Again, there is theoretical philanthropy. One phase of this, the temperance movement, appealed to Moody very much, because of its intimate connection with general moral questions, and because it so often afforded dramatic illustrations of the power of regenerating religion. "I have an idea that this rum devil is the worst we have nowadays, and it takes just as much power to cast them out as it took to cast the devil out of this man. I think no other power will do it." [48] And elsewhere he says: "Once I got into a place where I had to get up and leave. I was invited into a home in the old country, and they had a late supper, and there were seven kinds of liquor on the table. I am ashamed to say they were Christian people. A deacon urged a young lady to drink until her face flushed. I got up from the table and went out —I felt that it was no place for me." [49] These passages are merely examples of Moody's constant outcry upon the subject.

Frances Willard's energy of protest could not go further. Yet even in regard to temperance Moody's fundamental attitude was· far different from that of Frances Willard. Read the whole striking account which Frances gives of her attempt to work with him. To her, temperance was religion, or at least it was the phase of religion in which she was wrapped up. To Moody the Christian religion was far more than even temperance. So long as Frances worked with him and according to his ideas, he welcomed her. But she was perfectly ready, for the sake of her cause, to go on to the same platform with those who denied the divinity of Christ. There Moody would not follow her. No matter how good the cause, it could not prosper with such advocates. And, says Frances, "Brother Moody's Scripture interpretations concerning religious toleration were too literal for me; the jacket was too strait—I could not wear it." [50]

When you come to more general philanthropy, where the moral connection is less obvious, Moody's detachment is much more marked. Even as to the actual relief of suffering, tender and sympathetic as he naturally was, the misery of the soul was so much more important than that of the body, that the latter was apt to be neglected, at least postponed. When he was most actively concerned with the hospital relief of the Civil War, this distinction in his conduct was marked. "Mr. Moody, full of the idea of saving souls, urged that the very first business in every case was to find out whether the sick or dying man were a child of God; if so, then it was not necessary to spend much time on him—he being safe enough already. If not, he was to be pointed at once to the Saviour." [51] No doubt this in itself did not mean the neglect of physical attendance, but evidently that was not the prime concern, as to some of us it would seem to be.

With reforms of a purely sociological nature, or where the material benefit is indirect and remote, that is, with general idealistic efforts to make a better and more habitable world, Moody has little sympathy and even little patience. He does not hesitate to find fault with abstract charity: "There is a good deal that we think is charity, that is really doing a great deal of mischief." [52] When the question of Woman's Suffrage intrudes, he expresses himself with decided bitterness: "Now, perhaps you women who belong to the Women's Christian Temperance Union may feel hurt, but I do think it is a master stroke of the devil when he gets you to stop to discuss women's rights." [53] And when the occasion demands, he does not hesitate to extend his protest much more widely: "I have heard of reform, reform, until I am tired and sick of the whole thing. It is regeneration by the power of the Holy Ghost that we need." [54]

In all this indifference and even antipathy to the reforming movements of this world there is no doubt fundamentally in Moody much the feeling suggested in Sainte-Beuve's remark as to the "invasion of philanthropy side by side with industrialism, which has secularized charity more and more and reduced it to material well-being for others and for oneself: which is not even the shadow of spiritual charity in the Christian sense." [55] But in Moody's case there were personal reasons added to the general attitude. To begin with, in spite of his sympathetic treatment of suffering that came close to him, his own rude and vigorous health rendered him, as so many others, but imperfectly sensitive to the subtler and more chronic forms of physical misery. His remark when some one fainted in a large meeting, though of course tactful and appropriate to the occasion, was not generally uncharacteristic: "Never mind that person who has fainted. Let us attend to the interests of our souls to-night." [56] In connection with this matter of physical suffering it is most notable that Moody's effort and influence never took the form of attempts to heal the sick. He performed no miracles along this line, and did not try to perform any.

Moreover, it is undeniable and natural that such intense preoccupation with the other world tends to undermine one's interest and one's useful activity in this. What happens here is utterly insignificant compared to what happens or will happen in heaven, and the effort to remedy merely temporary evils is too temporary and too trifling much to agitate a soul fixed upon the joys and sorrows of eternity. And with Moody there was this still further, most important point to be remembered. He lived in the constant hope and expectation of the end of the world. The Bible sayings as to the second coming of Christ were deeply registered in his memory, and if he did not cherish any definite creed of Second Adventism, there can be no doubt that he felt the desperate imminence of a convulsion in which all the things that most matter to man here would become of no moment and be utterly wiped out. The world was bad and irretrievably, inevitably getting worse. Why bother to dream of a pitiable botching of a bad job? Man, from a this-worldly point of view, was hopeless: "Man was a failure under the judges, a failure under the prophets, and now for two thousand years under grace he has been a most stupendous failure." [57] In a very striking record of a conversation with Moody, Beecher represents this point of view: "I thought I saw the secret of his working and plans. He is a believer in the second advent of Christ, and in our own time. He thinks it is no use to attempt to work for this world. In his opinion it is blasted —a wreck bound to sink—and the only thing that is worth doing is to get as many of the crew off as you can, and let her go." [58] When you look at things thus, when you feel that this world is pre-destined to destruction and to a speedy end, you naturally take little interest in the improvement of it. Furthermore, it must be always remembered that in an ideally perfect world there would have been little occupation for Moody.

IV

So it is clear that, in spite of his humanity, Moody was by habit and surroundings and by natural taste a minister, a priest. As we look back through the centuries, it is impossible to avoid the feeling that the priest everywhere forms a caste by himself, shut off from the rest of humanity by his office, his preoccupations, his mental attitude, and this separation continues to prevail to-day, if less externally obvious than in some centuries past. The minister may mingle freely with the world, he may make it his business to know the ways of men, to be, as he fondly imagines, all things to all of them. But they treat him as something remote, and with all his efforts, he feels himself to be so. As we have seen, in this country a hundred and fifty years ago the remoteness largely consisted in a vast sense of superiority tacitly assumed and recognized. The superiority has utterly vanished, but the remoteness remains.

It is most interesting in the variety of ministers to see the way in which two extreme types deal with this remoteness. One type, now rather rapidly vanishing, accepts the distance and almost takes comfort in it. There, is the quiet, saintly pastor, chiefly in the country districts, who is set apart from his flock by his thought as much as by his garb, and who looks upon the wild doings of the twentieth century with a tender astonishment and a more or less desperate effort to remedy ills which he does not in the least understand. Then, on the other side, there is the quick jaunty man of the world, who makes his dress that of

FOUR GENERATIONS OF THE MOODY FAMILY.

Showing Grandma Moody, D. L. Moody, W. R. Moody and his child Irene Moody.

MR. MOODY'S MOTHER, DIED 1896, IN HER NINETY-FIRST YEAR.

trivial everyday life, and tries to make his spiritual attitude as much as possible the same. He jokes and tells stories, smokes and plays cards, cultivates always an air of polite, jovial ease and immense familiarity with the wicked world which he is supposed to be endeavoring to save. Nobody would ever take him for a minister, he feels, unless when he himself thinks proper solemnly to assert the fact. Alas, he is quite mistaken. Everybody knows him, everybody who has to meet him treats him as exactly what he is. I take the following striking words from the "Confessions of a Confessor," written some years ago, by a minister who fully realized the nature and the width of the unbridgeable gap: "He cannot associate on terms of equality with his fellows; they refuse to have it so. They refuse either to meet him on his own ground or to let him meet them on theirs. The great majority of people either look up to him, or look down on him; and both attitudes alike must cause him pain." [59]

Now it will naturally be said that Moody, by his immense and splendid humanity, and by his lack of formal consecration, should escape this ministerial remoteness altogether. He does not; to my feeling he does not escape it at all. He is a priest all the time, and as a man among men you cannot touch him, or only imperfectly. I feel the ministerial atmosphere about him. The jokes, no matter how boisterous, are those of ministers. The faces are those of ministers, as I see them arrayed in volume after volume, long faces, round faces, whiskered faces, smooth faces, solemn faces, jovial faces, always those of ministers, till the type has somehow grown to be an obsession to me. Moody's own face has the soul-saver stamped all over it. I know that I should never have felt at ease with him. It would have been a shock like a shower-bath, to have a cordial, courteous, assiduous host suddenly drop on his knees, with a stentorian "let us pray," or assail me in the most genial moment with the staggering interrogatory, "Are you a Christian?"

All the same, it is true, as Drummond said, that Moody was a tremendous human, as he was tremendous every way. And by his humanity he won and retained a tremendous power for his purposes over other human beings, a power which will furnish matter for the next chapter.

CHAPTER VI

MOODY THE MAN OF BUSINESS

I

IT is evident that from an early stage of his activity Moody was a great leader of men. He could guide them, inspire them, control them. Whenever he had a practical object to accomplish in this world, he could secure helpers and followers, who would support and sustain him with energy, enthusiasm, money, to an almost unlimited extent.

He had an extraordinary power of finding, selecting, and winning the men who would answer his purposes, who were adapted to understand and execute them. As Dr. Goss says, "He instantly summoned men to assume grave responsibilities with no other knowledge of their fitness than his own unaided intuitions, the confidence which he reposed in these intuitions being as unquestioning, apparently, as that of an animal in its instincts." [1] A notable example of this instantaneous appreciation and selection we have already observed in the case of Sankey, but the same thing happened over and over again, perhaps not always with fortunate results, but often enough amply to prove the gift of the selector. No doubt the process of selection was an instinctive one, as Dr. Goss suggests, but the instinct sometimes formulated itself in slight but significant guiding principles. "When you shake hands with a man, look out for him if his hand is as limp as a dead fish." [2] Again, he warned against those who "tell all they know at first acquaintance." [3] Students of character know well that such principles are not absolute, but they know also that a fair amount of reliance can be placed upon them.

In the management of men, after they had been selected, Moody also worked by instinct, as the great masters do, and he worked with an admirable and almost unerring skill. When it was necessary to use tact, his supply of it was limitless. Take his own comment upon such methods. He was once asked how it was possible to get along in a church where there were two Scotch elders who were at odds, so that one wouldn't take part if the other did. His answer was "Ask them to tea with you, and if there is any difference get it out of the way. . . . The best man you can have in a church is a Scotchman, if he is headed

MOODY THE MAN OF BUSINESS

right, and you can afford to spend some time to get him right if he is wrong." [4]

He not only recommended the methods, he applied them, with a gentle suavity and winning grace, which made men feel that they were above all things anxious to do what he wished, that what he wished was inevitably the best thing to do. Read the account by Dr. Grenfell of his brief interview with the evangelist, who inquired about his experiences in Labrador. Then Moody asked: "Could you come and tell them at the afternoon service in the Tremont Temple in three minutes?" And Grenfell smiled, but answered: "I can try." "Then I'll be grateful if you'll do so. Side door at three-thirty. Good-by. Ever so many thanks for dropping in." And Grenfell adds: "There was no unctuousness, no snobbery, no cant; and yet again he had moved my heart to want to do things more than ever." [5] Even with men who differed from him, who did not take any great interest in his religious views and arguments, the power was much the same. If he undertook to show them that something must be done and that they could help do it, they helped gladly.

When it was a question not of tact, but of straight persuasion by argument, he was equally ready and successful. The most noted instance of this is perhaps the session of ministers in London, who examined him thoroughly as to his doctrines and views, to see if they were willing to give him their support. His answers were quiet and respectful; but they were so alert and cogent that even the most lukewarm found it difficult to resist them.

And as he was gentle and persuasive in winning men, so he was equally gentle and considerate in using them. With all his own enormous, inexhaustible power of work, he appreciated that others were not so solidly built, and he was ready to relax the tension at any time, when he felt that they might not hold out. As Dr. Stebbins puts it: "He was ever thoughtful of those helping him, however, as it is my pleasure to testify, for he would say to me at the close of a heavy day's work just before beginning his last sermon for the day: 'You slip out and go home, for I want you to be fresh for to-morrow.'" [6]

But if Moody could employ tact and argument, he could also be immensely and even roughly arbitrary, if the occasion required it. When he was told that there might be resistance to some of his projects and that argument would not answer, his favorite phrase was, "Then we must roll them over." He rolled them over without hesitation. A satirist gives a vivid picture of some of his methods with his subordinates: "He came and looked over the Tabernacle with the eye of an expert in stage properties. He heard of Brother Webb's little envelope trick and said peremptorily, 'Stop it!' Then he whispered in Brother Pentecost's ear, 'Git!' And Pentecost put on his sea boots and walked. He wanted to take up another collection first, but Moody would have none of it."[7] Equally striking accounts come from more friendly sources. In the very early days, Moody arranged with an agent for a series of meetings in a certain school house. "All very well," said the man, "but who is to conduct them?" "You are." "I?" said the man. "I never did such a thing in my life." "Then it is time you did," was Moody's answer. The man conducted the meetings and successfully.[8] Again, in later years Dr. Torrey ventured to remonstrate at some arrangement which seemed to him ill-judged. Moody simply replied: " 'You do as you are told,' and I did as I was told; that is the way I kept my job."[9]

If it seems matter for surprise that men submitted to such arbitrary treatment, the answer is, first that they were convinced of Moody's absolute sincerity and unselfishness, second, that he had the supreme gift of inspiring a belief in his success. No doubt this was in part bred and strengthened by the fact that he did succeed and go on succeeding. But more than that, there was the sense of power which made men lean back upon him. Where he led they were willing to go, and they obeyed his orders, because they were confident that the orders were right. In commenting upon this remarkable influence, Dr. Goss almost wonders whether there was not something hypnotic about it. He even asks Moody the question, to be received with scorn, as might have been expected. "Not if I know myself. If I thought my influence was owing to that, I would quit preaching to-morrow. Any power I have comes from the Spirit of God." [10]

As Moody could win men, so he could make them work. This is perhaps the greatest secret of executive genius. So many men of excellent ability can do things themselves, but cannot ensure their being done by others or in the right way, and so do not trust others to undertake them. Moody had the instinct of judging a man's powers and setting him to the task for which he was fitted. As we saw above, in the case of one who had never conducted a meeting, he made men discover themselves, find out in their own natures powers they had never suspected. Nothing increases a man's respect for himself or his usefulness like that. Moreover, ardently intent as Moody was on his own plans and purposes, he was always remarkably ready to let others do their tasks in their own way, and he was eager to get suggestions from them as to a better way than his. Says one of his followers: "It was this openness to new ideas and responsiveness to new plans which did much to give him such a strong hold on growing, studying, ambitious young men." [11] Perhaps also he was not wholly insensible to the practical advantage of having your plans carried out by others, in that if the plans fail, others often get the blame, and if they succeed, the credit comes to you. But there is no evidence that this advantage was ever abused by Moody.

In the gift of far-seeing organization and preparation Moody was notable. True, he said of himself that he was a creature of impulse, [12] but his impulses were the product of an intuition and a broad grasp which were as comprehensive as they were unerring. He could tear his way through red tape and long-established conventions; but when these things served his turn, nobody could make better use of them. One thing that shows his strong executive instinct was his contempt for the mania for committees, that device for halving both responsibility and efficiency, which is the curse of American politics. "We don't want committees," he said. "When you want anything done, tell Mr. So-and-so to do it, and you will accomplish something. One is enough to constitute any committee. If there had been a committee appointed, Noah's ark would never have been built." [13]

Impulsive as he was, when he had a far-reaching project to carry out, he could wait and consult and deliberate, get the best plans from others that they were capable of, and then out of them form a better of his own. His revivals were successful because they were carefully engineered, and every detail considered before a step was taken. As a contemporary observer, quoted by Mr. Duffus, describes it: "The Hippodrome work is a vast business enterprise, organized and conducted by business men, who put their money into it on business principles, for the purpose of saving souls." [14] George Adam Smith's record of what Moody himself told him of the preparation for his first great English campaign well illustrates the care, the system, the forethought with which all his great triumphs were achieved: "He himself told me a wonderful thing. He had made, I think, at least two visits to our country in order to study the situation. He had come to hear our preachers and to watch their effects. He had made himself familiar with the salient tendencies of our popular religion and with the wants of the people outside the churches." [15] When impulse is supplemented by intelligent, disciplined effort like that, it gets somewhere.

II

It is sometimes said that in using human agents for his purposes, Moody was inclined to treat them as agents merely, to take them up when he needed them and to drop them with equal readiness, and I have quoted a passage to this effect in connection with Sankey. The same is true of all really great executive spirits. They have a task to perform which is more than any man's susceptibilities. As was well said of Moody's predecessor, Wesley, he "had extensive and well-defined plans for doing good; and he had a heart which could deliberately sacrifice every interest and every feeling, either of himself or his friends, that stood in the way of their accomplishment." [16] Moody's profound personal loyalty to those he loved is indisputable. Further, no criticism from outside sources could shake his persistent use of those in whom he believed. The cardinal illustration of this is Drummond. Drummond's views in some respects were far different from Moody's, so different that many persons objected to his appearance on the Northfield platform at all. Moody felt that Drummond had more of Christ's spirit than all the critics put together, and he paid no attention to their remonstrances. There were numerous similar examples. At the same time, there is Dr. Goss's hardly disputed charge that "when he dropped men it was as if they were 'hot coals' and it was impossible for those from whom he had received such loyal and almost passionate devotion at one time not to feel as if he were unkind and untrue when he turned away." [17] Yet, Dr. Goss also supplies the explanation, which is as with Wesley. The man was serving a cause, which was above all human considerations, and, as Dr. Atkins points out, most of those who were discarded were ready to perceive this; "and they were willing to be used by him or discarded by him, because they had been fired with a like love for the same cause." [18]

But, though Moody could usually have his own way and could dominate most men, it was inevitable that he should at times meet friction and opposition. How did he take it? It appears that in the main his spirit was singularly large, sweet, and conciliatory. There is none of the bitterness of Wesley's quarrels with Whitefield, nothing of Wesley's bitter outcry against his fellow-workers; "I have not one preacher with me and not six in England whose wills are broken to serve me thus." [19] Kindly and large-minded as General Booth was, he could declare in a moment of temper: "I will never forgive the Baptists, neither in this world nor the world to come." [20] Moody had his own good hot temper to fight with, in his youth, at any rate, but there is no mention in his case of any such outbreak as this. Nor does he seem ever to have developed the tendency to suspicion or querulousness that appears in the complaint of Finney: "I learned from various sources that a system of espionage was being carried on that was destined to result in an extensive union of ministers and churches to hedge me in and prevent the spread of the revivals in connection with my labors." [21] Moody was far too broad, too genial, too wise ever to become the victim of obsessions of this nature.

It is indeed said by some that with years he grew a trifle overbearing and disposed to lecture instead of persuade, and in some of his later evangelistic campaigns this tendency is believed to have hampered his usefulness. But I imagine that if such a tendency existed, it was the result of his mistrust of the so-called liberalizing movement in the church which to him seemed insidious and disastrous and totally opposed to the fundamental principles of salvation. At any rate, through all his life from beginning to end there was a desire to conciliate, a passionate effort for harmony, and a sense of the utter necessity of it in face of the encroaching dominion of evil, which are as gentle and tender as they are noble and disarming. Over and over again instances are recorded like the following: "At a certain meeting for the promotion of a revival, one good brother rose and criticised him severely for his uncharitableness, when Mr. Moody said with deep emotion, 'From my heart I thank that brother. I deserved it. Will you, my brother, pray for me?'" [22] There is no trace of cant in this: it is the self-reproach and self-confession of a great spirit. And at the bottom of it is the underlying feeling which is so apt to be absent in promoters and creators and which appears so fully in Moody's remark, after listening to several hours of futile wrangling: "Mac, the world is in great need of peace-makers." [23] He felt it to be so, and for all he was a magnificent fighter, he was minded to be a peace-maker himself.

The interesting question as to Moody's power over men is, how far he was conscious of it and how far he deliberately enjoyed it. There is no real evidence that the power puffed him up or made him vain. As in so many other connections, there is no sign whatever of self-analysis on the point, of his interrogating himself as to what the nature of his power was or as to the satisfaction it might give or any dangers involved in that satisfaction. If you asked him, he would instantly have asserted that such power as he had was wholly God's gift and would abandon him in a moment if he ceased to use it for God's service. Yet it is well known that there is no higher intoxication in the world than just this power over men and the sense that you can lead them as you will, when you will, whither you will. There can be no doubt that Moody felt the intoxication and that it was the breath of life to him. The world, his world, and his was a big world, came and went as he told it to, men took their orders from him and obeyed them without question. Those who managed and arranged his meetings and carried on his institutions were under his direction, and from top to bottom his guiding hand was felt in everything. Who that was equal to such power could have failed to enjoy it? Probably few men have ever enjoyed it more than D. L. Moody.

And then one asks oneself about the converse of the proposition: did this master of command ever learn to obey? As to obedience to other men the question hardly arises. All his life he was a leader and a law unto himself. He planned, arranged, decided; it was for others to execute. The mere conception of taking orders unhesitatingly, of surrendering his will without dispute to the will of another, would have been so utterly foreign to him that it is doubtful whether it would have had any meaning. It is, to be sure, urged that in his youthful service with his uncle, he was found obedient; but I imagine that even then there was more adaptation verging into dictation than unarguing obedience. It is urged that in his relations with others he was supremely humble, recognized the directions in which he was inferior and was apt and eager to learn. It is, as we have seen, repeatedly urged that he was willing to stand aside and put others forward when he felt that they could do the work better than he. All this is true enough. But in every bit of it he retained control of himself, of his purposes, of his agents, and the apparent resignation of power only made the fundamental retention of it all the sweeter. No: if he had ever met a man whom he really felt to be bigger than himself, he might have been prepared to obey him unhesitatingly. But I do not think he ever met such a man, and he would have had to go some way to find one.

There remains something very different from obedience to man, and that is obedience to God. On the surface it appears that Moody was one who obeyed the will of God so absolutely that he had no existence independent of that motive force. This is most emphatically insisted upon by others. *"He was a fully surrendered man,"* says Dr. Torrey; "every ounce of that two-hundred-and-eighty-pound body of his belonged to God." [24] Moody himself is equally positive. Of one of the great struggles of his life he declared: "The best thing

I ever did was when I surrendered my will, and let the will of God be done in me." [25] 'And again, more generally, and more vigorously: "If I know my own mind, if an angel should come from the throne of God and tell me that I could have my will done the rest of my days on earth, and that everything I wished should be carried out, or that I might refer it back to God, and let God's will be done in me and through me, I think in an instant I would say: 'Let the will of God be done.'" [26]

Yet one wonders. Was the Will of God ever distinct from the will of D. L. Moody? God's will was mysterious, obscure. The will of Moody was always crisply definite, all-engrossing. Might it not be strangely, perilously easy, to substitute one for the other, so that a convenient, overmastering exchange was taking place all the time? There is a profound sentence which Fénelon wrote to Madame de Maintenon and which may find its place here: "The I, of which I have so often written to you, is an idol which you have not broken. You desire with all your heart to enter into God, but not by the gate of the I; on the contrary, you seek in God to find your I." [27] The I is so intrusive, so insinuating, so insidious, so enormous!

And the strands of obedience and domination, of arrogance and humility, of self-assertion and self-surrender are so strangely interwoven in the complex fabric of the human heart!

III

As Moody was a master of men, so he was a magnificent master of money. Again and again you feel in him the thorough-going, solid, commercial instinct of the Anglo-Saxon man of business and affairs. It is even undeniable that a certain suggestion of this attitude enters into his religion. To be sure, he tries to be on his guard: "Let us make no bargains with the Lord, but be ready to go out and do whatever he appoints." [28] Yet the Lord will appear as a man of business and it is your business to make the best bargain with him you can, or let Moody do it for you: "If a lady goes shopping, she wants to get the best ribbon she can for the money. If a man wants a coat he wants to get the best coat he can for the money. This is the law the world around. If we show men that religion is better than anything else, we shall win the world." [29] It is the dialect of the shoe-trade, and there is no doubt that it is mighty and prevailing.

Moody was skilled in large financial organization. Here, as in everything, he was a systematizer, looked far ahead both to needs and resources, planned to adapt them to each other, and saw to it that his plans would and did work out. Perhaps he lacked the advantage of early experience in minute detail of personal accounts, and sometimes let minor matters slip. Frances Willard gives an amusing description of his utterly neglecting to provide for her expenses and leaving her to shift for herself after he had expressly engaged her.[30] But in the larger conception of problems and methods his command was perfect and really astonishing. He would attempt what others did not dream of and carry out what others dared not attempt.

It must be admitted that he was a shrewd, keen, careful, and successful bargainer. Here, as always, the first emphasis must be placed upon his scrupulous honesty. It is unfortunately true that in the business world there is a certain prejudice against persons of religious affiliation, and the prejudice may not be wholly without grounds. We may assume that lack of practical training enters into the matter. But there have been too many cases of men who stood eminently well with

God, at least in their own opinion, but whose
financial methods were somewhat shady. There is
no trace of evidence associating Moody with any
such methods whatever. On the contrary, he
seems to have been always anxious to avoid misrepresentation or fraud and to stand behind any
transaction that he was involved in with all the
money and all the credit he had.

But he had the Yankee love for a good bargain.
In his early Sunday School days, he said to his
teacher: "Moses was smart, wasn't he?" You
couldn't say more for Moses. When Moody was
young and in the shoe trade, it is said that it was
the custom if "sharp or unmanageable men or
women came in to buy, to turn them over to
Moody, who took great delight in dealing with
them on that very account." [31] And they did not
get ahead of him, far from it. "Nothing was ever
misrepresented in the smallest particular; but
when it came to a question of sharpness of wit between buyer and seller, Moody generally had the
best of it." [32] He had that inimitable bargainer's
instinct, which is the root of all successful trading,
of knowing just exactly how far to go yourself,
and divining exactly how far the other fellow can
be made to go. The instinct never failed him till

death and he enjoyed a good trade, quite independent of its helping on the Kingdom of Heaven, although he was always careful to see that it turned that way.

This financial instinct naturally brought Moody into close relations with the other great masters of money. Big men on Wall Street and in the English financial centers appreciated him, admired him, liked him, trusted him. He met them as an equal, and dictated to them when he saw fit. A certain great financier was asked: "How is it that while you and other like men are all but inaccessible, fenced in by closed doors and guarded by polite but immovable private secretaries, Dwight L. Moody sees you at any time?" "He is one of us," was the reply.[33] Obviously such an intimacy had its dangers. One of them lay in the charge that was frequently brought in connection with Billy Sunday. It was said that these financiers were glad to subsidize religion like Moody's because it made the poor contented in this world and allowed the rich to go on pillaging and plundering undisturbed. Of course Moody would have resented such an insinuation instantly. At the same time, his peculiar indifference to this-worldly conditions made him in some respects exceptionally liable to it. And there is the further suggestion that the millionaire was buying his way into heaven, and that he could obtain from the evangelist a sweet security as to his future by atoning for his misdeeds with large cash payments here. On this point also one anticipates Moody's protest. What were financiers to him but sinners fleeing damnation like all others? Could any one suppose for a moment that he would flatter them or truckle to them any more than to other sinners? Probably he did nothing of the kind. Yet the danger was there, and I cannot help recalling the remark of General Booth: "I have been trying all my life to stretch out my arms so as to reach with one hand the poor and at the same time to keep the other in touch with the rich. But my arms are not long enough. I find that when I am in.touch with the poor I lose my hold upon the rich, and when I reach up to the rich I let go of the poor." [34] The cry of tainted money was perhaps not quite so prominent in Moody's day as it became a little later. No doubt in that day and in all days he would have refused absolutely to have anything to do with money or anything else that seemed to him tainted. But he had unlimited confidence in his reasoning powers, and reason brings about some astonishing results.

In any case, Moody had vast ingenuity in getting money for his own causes and also for those of others. His ingenuity was so inexhaustible, his shrewdness, his keenness, his adaptability, so varied and so surprising, that one is almost tempted to say that if Moody's God had been half so clever as Moody, we should be living in a better world. Again it is necessary to repeat the insistence upon the man's perfect honesty and sincerity. There was never any misrepresentation, any pretense of doing things that could not be done and never were done. It was precisely because of the universal confidence in his integrity and straightforwardness that men were ready to help; so that one authority justly points out that he could get a million dollars where others could not get a thousand.[35]

In money-getting there was first the tireless activity that appeared in everything else. Money must be had: "We must ask for money, *money,* MORE MONEY, at every meeting; not for the support of the Association—as it now is—but to enlarge its operations." [36] Very well, if money was needed, go out and seek it. It would not come to you, you must go to it, and keep going, with an insistence that knew no fatigue and no discouragement.

But the energy would go but little way without

the help of God. When the undertaking was wise and worth while, God would surely help, if you asked Him, and the way was to ask earnestly, repeatedly, and hopefully. Sometimes the results were astonishing. On one occasion twenty thousand dollars were needed for the Northfield Schools. Moody did not tell a soul who could possibly assist him about the matter. "But," says Dr. Torrey, "he looked right to God and said: 'I need twenty thousand dollars for my work; send me that money in such a way that I will know it comes straight from Thee.' And God heard that prayer. The money came in such a way that it was clear that it came from God, in direct answer to prayer." [37]

Besides work and prayer, Moody had methods of his own that no one else thought of or practiced so successfully. When others considered that they had been working and had done their little best, he would take hold and make their results seem petty enough. There was a Scotch minister, an able and prominent man, who was laboring industriously but modestly to get money for some special purpose. Moody came along and was impatient. It would take all winter to do anything that way, he said. He started one day with the minister to visit a certain rich woman.

"How much will you ask for?" said Moody. "Oh, perhaps fifty pounds." Moody made no comment, but when they reached the house, he pushed forward and said to the lady: "Madam, we have come to ask you for two thousand pounds to help build the new Mission." She threw up her hands in horror. "Oh, Mr. Moody, I cannot possibly give you more than one thousand." [38] That was the way he did it.

He would not take no, he would not give up. When he was starting with Sankey for England, there was no money, but he went ahead with all his preparations, and the money came. Endless, unfailing, unconquerable persistence was his asset, one of them, and we all know that few forms of capital bear better interest. Read how he alone turned a Sunday School Convention, which had been a palpable failure, into a success, simply by passionate urging that failure was impossible. [39] And his own fruitful comment on such matters was: "What we want is to turn defeat into victory. If a man can't do that, he is a failure." [40]

IV

Moody lived in the age which invented American publicity, and he was a close contemporary of Barnum, who may be said to have been as much the inventor of publicity as any one man. It was not newspaper publicity alone, which made Barnum's reputation and success, but the further attempt, doubtless suggested by the vogue of the newspaper, to arouse and stimulate and sharpen public interest and curiosity in every possible way.

Barnum's methods of advertising were no doubt often open to question. So the appeal was effective, he was not always too scrupulous as to its truth. No human being could charge that Moody, in his efforts to advertise, was any more unscrupulous or dishonest than in any other branch of activity. It is true that his enemies sometimes made capital of these efforts, and pushed the analogy with Barnum as far as possible. "Do you want to know the secret of Moody's success?" writes one critic. "Well, read Barnum's 'Humbugs of the World.' Moody is perfect master of the philosophy of that book." [41] And a much more kindly and sympathetic observer protests to some extent: "That Mr. Moody's keen business sense should have effectively arranged and advertised the movement is creditable to his religious purpose as well as to his sagacity. The advertising has certainly been very thorough and in some respects distasteful and oppressive to us; but Mr. Moody's work could not begin until attention was drawn to it, and to say that he succeeds is to say that he is not fastidious." [42]

These strictures did not disturb Moody in the least. He had the greatest thing in the world, not to sell, but to give away, and he was determined by every honest means to let the world know its opportunity. Everything that print and paint and light and noise would do was legitimate, if only it really served its object. I have quoted in an earlier chapter his device of having thousands of handbills printed and getting his young men to circulate them about the streets. One should read further his account of the foreigner who could not speak a word of English and to whom the bills were given for distribution. He had to be dealt with by an interpreter. "But when the Lord converted him, the man was so happy! His face was just lit up, and to every man that went by—and there were some pretty hard cases—he just gave a handbill. And some thanked him and some swore at him, but he kept smiling all the time. He couldn't tell the difference between thanks and curses." [43]

Later imitators and emulators have so far outgone Moody in this matter of publicity for salvation that his methods seem comparatively tame. But his energetic defense and explanation of them is too characteristic and significant to be missed. When he was asked if he believed in advertising, his answer was: "Certainly I do. Why not? I don't see why we shouldn't learn something from the world. They advertise very extensively. A man comes into town from the country or from some other city, and he don't know anything about the meetings, and if he sees a notice of them he may attend them. I don't see why the walls should not be placarded also. Many a man has been blest in that way. Some people are sensitive about it, I know; but it seems to me it is a good deal better to advertise and have a full house than to preach to empty pews. I don't see why not. Bills are stuck up everywhere for people to go to theaters and places of amusement, and I don't see why we shouldn't give the Gospel a chance." [44]

Moody's relation to the newspaper as a special form of publicity is peculiarly interesting. We have seen how bitter was his dislike of the Sunday papers, and in the same way the daily papers printed much that he could not possibly approve. Moreover, while on the whole the more intelligent journals treated him usually with forbearance and often with active and helpful support, giving largely of their space to his discourses, and adding comment of a nature to enlist the attention of their readers, he had also to endure a good deal of rough satire and even slanderous abuse. When the attacks were confined to his personality, his uncouthness, his lack of education and manners, he was quite indifferent. But when the purity of his motives was questioned, he was sometimes annoyed, and more often grieved and seriously troubled. Yet, after all, he knew well what the power of the newspapers was, knew how much they could help him and how much they had helped him, and as late as 1897 he had an enthusiastic word about them: "I want to speak a word for the papers. They are a great help to us. Buy papers. Buy lots of them. They are for sale. Religious people grumble about the newspapers and say they don't give enough space to sermons. When a good sermon is printed, buy that paper. Buy them by the hundred, and scatter them broadcast." [45]

With the human embodiment of journalism, the reporter, Moody's attitude was much the same as with the newspaper in the abstract. He realized the reporter's power, and was good-natured, friendly, and conciliating with him where it was possible to be so. Also, the reporter had a soul to be saved like anybody else, and it was desirable to save it, if one could. But it was so thoroughly wrapped up in newspaper that it was difficult to get at. And any way, the fellows were so critical, so impersonal, and so everlastingly curious, merely curious, that you could not get a hold upon them, while their deplorable taste for sensationalism and excitement, even at the expense of veracity, made it necessary to be on one's guard. People accuse us revivalists of working by excitement, he says, but we are not the only ones: "Newspapers can say nothing. If there is anybody under the sun that tries to get up sensations, it is the reporter. If there isn't any sensation in sight, he makes one. He is the last that should throw stones at us." [46]

With the more personal aspect of publicity, the inclination to put oneself and one's own affairs before the community at large, Moody had little patience. Many notable people profess to shrink from this, but I really think his shrinking was sincere. When Dr. Goss asked him why he refused to have his name connected with a particular church, he replied: "Why? Because I am no more than any other man. And besides, who knows but that I may do something to disgrace it?" [47] Again, as to the writing of his biography he said: "I do not know of anything that can be said of my life that would interest people." "And yet," adds Dr. Goss, "within two years after that letter was written, he told me with his own lips that he could sell his biography at any moment for $25,000, and that when he was in New York he was offered $10,000 for a two hours' interview by an agent of one of the great newspapers." [48] In the same way he fled the camera, so zealously that it was often difficult to get photographs for proper purposes of illustration. When his pictures and Sankey's were hawked about the streets, he protested: "I don't know that anything is hindering the work more than these men that are making money out of us. If you want hymnbooks, go into some bookstore and buy them. Don't buy these photographs. They are no more photographs of us than they are of you." [49] The truth is, he was too big for petty vanity, and really to shun newspaper prominence a man has to be very big indeed.

V

With this immense and solid grasp on human action and the practical agencies of this world, one sometimes wonders why Moody did not leave behind him a much more definite and tangible impress. Preachers of less power than he have founded sects to bear their names. He left no sect and no distinctive body of followers. Neither did he leave any world-wide, permanent organization to be his monument, as the Salvation Army

CROSSLEY HALL MOUNT HERMON

MOUNT HERMON SCHOOL COTTAGES

A PAGE FROM MR. MOODY'S BIBLE.

is the monument of General Booth. Perhaps Booth, while he had a no more puissant personality than Moody, was an even more systematic and especially a more definitely persistent organizer. But it is justly urged in Moody's favor that his natural breadth and tolerance made him wholly unwilling to confine his teaching or his influence within the narrow limits of a sect or an organization. Moreover, it is not at all certain that the depth of his spiritual influence was not more permeating and more permanent, if less intensely personal, than if he had associated it with a peculiar religious body.

He did, however, leave behind him a group of institutions which have perpetuated his memory with a significant and far-reaching influence, the educational institutions to which he gave so much of his time and thought during the latter portion of his life. The Boys' School at Mount Hermon, just across the river from Moody's home in Northfield, the Girls' School in Northfield itself, the Bible Institute in Chicago, and the Northfield yearly summer Conferences, are surely, each and all of them monuments by which any man might be proud to have his name transmitted to posterity. The schools were intended by Moody to furnish intellectual, practical, and above all spiritual training for boys and girls, often young men and women, to whom, for various reasons, the ordinary forms of education were less easily accessible. The Bible Institute was primarily established for the more thorough training of lay religious workers. And the Northfield Conferences gathered and still gather together men of distinction from America and Europe to study and discuss the great religious problems of the world in the largest and freest spirit. It was especially in connection with these that Moody's broad tolerance was manifest. If a man was earnestly working for the Lord, no matter whether his way was Moody's way or not, he was eagerly invited to Northfield to tell them about it.

In all respects Moody devoted his splendid powers of inspiration and management to the establishing and maintaining of these institutions. The schools especially, being run right at his own door, were his pet interest and he could not do enough for them. Money? He could get unlimited money. All he had to do, in America or England, was to go out and ask for it, and it came. Teachers? Courses of study? Athletics? He watched all these with intense interest, and was always ready with suggestions, which were often novel and useful, sometimes surprisingly so, considering how little educational experience he had had himself. And yet the distinct testimony is, that, in spite of his constant interest, he did not interfere or hamper his subordinates in any way. Oh, he would occasionally telephone and suggest that it was a fine day and he might look in and mightn't the boys and girls celebrate by having a holiday. But in general, as with everything, his habit was to get helpers whom he could trust, men and women who knew their business thoroughly, and then leave them to do it, with none of that nagging criticism and suspicion which make executive efficiency so difficult, if not impossible.

What is most interesting about his attitude is his enthusiasm for education generally. We have seen that he himself had little of a formal nature. We have seen that in some respects he mistrusted it. It is then rather fine and striking and indicative of largeness of spirit that he should have made it one of the chief efforts of his life to propagate in others what had been so emphatically omitted in himself. To be sure, it has often been noted that those have generally most enthusiasm for education who know least about it, while those whose contact with it has been most solid and extensive come most to realize how little it can improve natural ability or sharpen natural dullness. Still, there is no question but that Moody's zeal was tempered with intelligence and directed with sure persistence to wise and worthy ends.

Also, perhaps he was as much interested, all the time, in the corrective or even the antidote for education, as in the thing itself. He felt strongly that in many modern schools and colleges mere knowledge was more and more sought after, to the utter neglect of what was to him the one thing needful. His schools were to supply the best of modern thought, to be thoroughly up-to-date in all modern methods and equipment, to have teachers who should be trustworthy guides through all the complicated mazes. But above all the things of God should be taught, the Word of God should be the foundation, and the men and women who went out from his portals should maintain and spread through the world the doctrines which he had given his whole passionate life to propagate. It is said that "his prayer at the laying of the cornerstone of one of the buildings was that God would wipe the school from the face of the earth if anything was taught here contrary to the Word of God." [50] Such an attitude is of course susceptible of many interpretations, and how far it can be permanently carried out depends upon the vitality of the doctrines to which Moody clung with his whole soul.

It is possible, however, that his insight into the real problems of education was deeper than many might suppose. In an earlier chapter I have developed at some length the view that our age is an age of ignorance. Naturally this blight of ignorance has made itself felt in the world of education more than anywhere else. The old idea of a liberal education, of a simple, solid body of knowledge which must be infused into all educated people and which forms a common basis for their communication with each other, has vanished, never to return. Familiarity with the Greek and Latin classics now merely isolates the few who possess it. But when it comes to a substitute for the older idea, we flounder in chaos, hopelessly astray. Before we decide how we are to get an education, we must decide what it is, and that no man at present knows. In despair over ignorance, over the utter failure and incompleteness of the intellectual side, many of us are turning for the solution to the practical. In default of the knowing, which is beyond us, we are looking to the doing, which is essential if we are to live at all.

In many respects this would seem to be the simple, sane way of dealing with the problem. Only, doing in itself is so apt to degenerate into the merely practical, the material, which looks to the immediate satisfactions of life, which substitutes bread and butter and automobiles altogether for the things of the spirit. Long ago Mary Lyon, when she founded Mount Holyoke, foresaw this difficulty. Though she was an educator, she was not a scholar any more than Moody was, and the mere hopeless labor of indefinite intellectual acquisition did not appeal to her. She did not want her girls to be scholars only, to accumulate vain learning for their own glorification. Neither did she want them to be mere practical drudges or material enjoyers. Her solution of the problem has a certain splendor from its very vagueness, and perhaps just because of that vagueness, it has a stimulating value which is lacking in more precise formulas. Her ideal, she said, was that her girls "should live for God and do something." [51] I think that Moody would have been perfectly content to inscribe that motto over the doors of his schools, and I do not know that he could have found a better one.

After this minute examination, in which we have seen Moody's mighty and magnificent powers in the management of his fellow human beings, one is tempted to wonder what he could have done if he had used those powers in the things of this world. In business, in politics, in administration of any kind, it seems as if insight into character like his, power of organization like his, above all the supreme gift of making men do what you wanted them to do and do it with the best that was in them, might have brought him to the very top. But he cared for nothing of the sort, and so we shall never know what his achievement might have been. After all, when our life here seems nothing but a bubble, a dream, a shadow, it is natural that one's ambition should concentrate less upon governing and managing men in this world than upon leading them into another. It is time now to turn our attention in more detail to Moody's methods of asserting and applying such leadership.

CHAPTER VII

THE MOLDER OF SOULS

I

THE power of molding souls is the greatest power in the world. In the preceding chapter we have seen how richly Moody possessed this power and how he used it to accomplish his purposes, so far as this world is concerned. But to use the power over others to influence them directly and for their own good is a subtler and more delicate task, and in performing this also Moody was a master.

In the chapter on "The Preacher" we dealt with Moody's influence over others in the mass. But even the mass was made up of individuals, and everywhere and at all times the individual was what preëminently interested him. As we have seen, his preaching was apt to be addressed to individuals, and he would pick out this or the other person in the audience, and fire his quick words right at him. This was carried so far that it has been suggested that the victims were sometimes prearranged beforehand and were special subjects for dramatic appeal.[1] I have found no evidence to show this in regard to Moody, and it is at any rate certain that he descended to no such cheap management of effect as has been practiced by some of his successors. But he did have in high degree the power of making individuals in his audience feel that he was speaking to them as if they were alone and as if he knew every inmost secret of their hearts. He could produce exactly the effect that Finney aimed at when he cried: "Do not think I am talking about anybody else; but I mean you, and you, and you."[2]

At the same time Moody never leaned very heavily upon public confession and testimony. In the older revivals one of the most striking features was the "Anxious Seat," a portion of the auditorium set apart for those who were in peculiar distress about their souls' condition and were peculiarly apt and ready to seize the proffered means of mercy. The psychological pressure exerted upon these conspicuous candidates for salvation was obviously as intense as it was artificial, and it was extremely difficult to resist. In consequence the confessions and conversions obtained though often dramatic enough, were less likely to be permanent than those brought about by a quieter, more direct, and more personal handling.

At any rate, this was Moody's view, and few men have had a more unerring instinct in such matters than he. He did not for a moment under-rate the force of mass influence, nor ever cease to work upon individuals collectively with all the means which he so well knew how to use. But the deep and enduring results were obtained by getting a man where you could look into his eyes and lay a quiet, controlling finger upon his arm, and so upon his heart.

In early New England revival effort, house to house visitation was a very marked feature. Where the power of the Church and the ministers was so great, such visitation assumed almost in-quisitorial proportions. According to Dewey's account: The women of the house being got to-gether "their inquisitors open with the most pointed questions, put in the most awful manner, concerning their most secret, solemn, and delicate feelings. . . . I have heard even intelligent fe-males declare that they never met with anything so horrifying as one of these visitations. And yet to resist one of them would mark out the family

that did it with the most signal reprobation." [3]
Of course nothing of this extreme character could
be carried out in any such fashion in Moody's day.
Still, I find the *Saturday Review's* comment on
what it calls "pious picketing" at the time of his
first visit to London almost as severe: "The pickets
are sometimes men, but as might be expected, more
commonly women. . . . They knock at the door
and ask to see the master or mistress . . . and on
any member of the family appearing, they are
assailed with questions which imply, and indeed
almost explicitly proclaim, a strong conviction on
the part of the visitor that those whom they are
addressing are altogether destitute of anything in
the nature of religion and probably doomed to
eternal perdition." [4]

I do not find Moody at any time energetically
practicing or instigating such methods as this,
though no doubt visitation in some form was and
is associated with revival effort, and there was always the unfailing formula, "Are you a Christian?" ready to hurl at any promising subject.
What he preferred, insisted on, and developed, was
the "Inquiry Room," the separate meeting-place in
which he could deal with those who had first been
stirred and affected by the sermon before the mul-

titude and could then be reached and touched when they were in a condition of intense susceptibility. He urges emphatically the value of this personal element: "Personal dealing is of the most vital importance. No one can tell how many souls have been lost through lack of following up the preaching of the Gospel by personal work. . . . People are not usually converted under the preaching of the minister. It is in the inquiry-meeting that they are most likely to be brought to Christ." [5] And this dealing must be man to man, soul to soul. There may be others about, but they must be attending to their own separate affairs, and the anxious convert must feel that he is opening his secrets to one other understanding heart and to that only. And Moody ridicules the mild suggestion of an incompetent minister that those who were troubled about their condition could appear before the church-committee: "Why, he might as well have asked them to go before a justice of the peace. Asking an awakened soul to go before the whole session! If you want to get these people to talk with you, put yourself in their way, and make it easy for them." [6] So for forty years, with ever-increasing experience, sureness, and skill he practiced the subtle science of reading and understanding men's souls and the exquisite art of guiding, and influencing them.

It is evident that the understanding and the influencing are two entirely different matters. For centuries legions of scholars and thinkers have devoted themselves to the business of understanding, without the slightest thought of any effort to influence. Modern psychology, with all its extensive apparatus of laboratories and measurements and questionnaires, is daily occupied with the effort to learn the nature and working of man's inner life, the origins and methods and objects of it. But before either the name or the practice of psychology was invented, the wisest of mankind had applied the utmost patience and the finest insight to the same object, and at times it seems with deplorably little result, a conclusion which some are disposed to echo in regard to even the achievements of recent psychology. Although it is not often appreciated, some of the chief masters of this science of soul have been the world's great dramatists and poets and novelists. They do not formulate their conclusions with the technical terminology of the laboratory, but for that very reason the conclusions are often less apt to be misleading; and the most delicate lessons of psychological observation are to be learned from Sophocles and Shakespeare, from Thackeray and Flaubert and Tolstoi and Anatole France. Again, the finest illustrations of soul-study may be derived from the great school of French critics of whom Sainte-Beuve was the acknowledged master and chief. Sainte-Beuve called himself a "Naturalist of Souls." In books and in life the thing above all others that interested him was the investigation of men's motives, the study of their hopes and aspirations and despairs. And if it seems far-fetched to associate such study as Sainte-Beuve's with such practice as Moody's, it must be remembered that some basis of instinctive study was the essential preliminary for Moody to obtain his results.

To Sainte-Beuve, however, the study was all. He never dreamed of influencing a single individual in any direction. The immense, the inexhaustible fascination of understanding was quite enough for him and others like him. But those who have the instinct for guidance, for control, find the understanding a mere basis for their work. Indeed, they are apt to be impatient of the intrusion of what seems to them mere curiosity in what they feel to be the deepest and most important concern of human life. With how much scorn does Saint Francis of Sales brand the indecent inquisition of these investigators who probe for their own amusement: "Many indulge in rash judgments for the pleasure of philosophizing and divining the characters of people as a mere intellectual exercise. If, by chance, they manage to hit the truth, their audacity and appetite for more increase so much, that it is almost impossible to turn them from the pursuit." Which would seem to dispose once for all of the passion of the biographer and psychographer. The real practitioners, the real artists in this kind, examine and analyze without end, but at every moment their analysis is turned to fruitful use in modifying, developing, almost creating human life.

In the Catholic Church the Confessional is of course the supreme agency by which this manipulation of souls is carried on. The Confessional had its inception in the early stages of Church discipline, but it was only by degrees and through centuries of discussion, and controversy that it became the highly developed instrument which is to-day, as it has so long been, at work affecting millions of souls. The skill, the tact, the infinite power of adaptation, which have been acquired in the long development of this spiritual agency are well suggested in the comment of a modern psychologist upon his conversation with one who understood and used it: "I once asked a Catholic priest how he dealt with certain adolescent religious difficulties. His reply showed that he had studied the whole question from the standpoint of physiology, psychology, and heredity, as well as theology, and that he varied his treatment of the cases according to the individual's symptoms. Some persons he controlled simply by authority; others he comforted as a mother soothes a restless infant; still others he sent to a physician. There, thought I, is one who has beheld the ideal of an art of religious culture drawn directly from scientific knowledge. How different is this from the ready-made methods that ignore differences of sex, of age, of disposition, and of physical condition." [7]

It is not necessary here to dwell upon the obvious dangers which have been so much emphasized in connection with the Confessional. The most prominent of these is the subjection of female penitents to a male confessor, and while the evils of this practice may have been exaggerated, they are undeniably very real. Almost as serious is the danger of turning over sensitive, anxious souls to management which is clumsy, tactless, and inadequate, and even with the best of training such a process is too often attended with disastrous results. But the supreme danger, as well as the supreme strength, of the Confessional lies in the fact that it appeals to an instinct of human nature so wide-spread, so deep-rooted, and so overwhelming, that not only the wise and the unselfish but the unscrupulous and the cunning too readily take advantage of it.

We all of us, in different degrees and in different fashions, long to confide our secrets to some one, if we could only find the right one. As Newman puts it: "How many souls are there in distress, anxiety, and loneliness, whose one need is to find a being to whom they can pour out their feelings unheard by the world. They want to tell them and not to tell them; they wish to tell them to one who is strong enough to hear them and yet not too strong to despise them." [8] How charmingly does Hawthorne make his Hilda, in "The Marble Faun," Hilda, the Puritan child of New England, in whom the horror of everything Catholic is inborn, turn in her distress to the Catholic Confessional in Saint Peter's and find soothing relief. It is perfectly well known that criminals ache with the longing to reveal what they have done, and that long-hidden evil deeds are finally uncovered in that way. Well, there are times when we are all criminals and know it. Again, we are just as eager to confide our good deeds as our naughty ones, to be praised for the former and comforted for the latter. The instinct of self-confession is fundamentally and universally human. Some persons who could never satisfy it by word of mouth will do it by letter, and will write long pages of intimate revelation to those with whom in actual presence such intimacy would be impossible. It is the same instinct that is at the bottom of much writing of journals and of elaborate autobiographies like Rousseau's and many another. The life which has been sternly repressed and hidden away during the earthly existence still longs somehow to leave a record of itself which some day some sympathetic soul may understand. In short, this impulse to confession is all a part of the unfailing, unconquerable, incurable, if utterly hopeless desire to escape from the eternally binding prison of ourselves.

It is not the Catholic priest alone who has to meet and deal with this self-confessing instinct. No priest of any creed has ever lived who has not had multitudes of sinners and sufferers beating at his doors in instant solicitation of the help and comfort which he is supposed to be able to administer. In Protestant countries, and especially in America, where the decay of priestly influence which I have insisted on has been so marked, a curious modification of this confessional recourse has taken place and the rôle of the priest has been largely assumed by the family physician. How many, many strange, pitiful, and terrible secrets have been poured into the country doctor's ears, and how many people have received from him not only the relief of confession but the further benefit of wise and strengthening guidance. It is one of the various unfortunate phases of the banishing of the old general practitioner by the specialist that this advantage of confessional comfort has largely disappeared. The busy, hurried, fashionable specialist, giving a few brief consultations by appointment, with a dozen other appointments crowding upon him, can never furnish that leisurely comfort and advice which were among the most useful functions of the medical profession. And yet I have had even specialists tell me that many a patient insisted upon confiding to them the most intimate personal matters entirely unconnected with the special malady which was supposed to be dealt with. And we have to remember always that the human desire for confession is immensely increased by pain and helplessness. As the lively lady in the comedy puts it: "When I am well, I don't go about telling the inmost longings of my soul, but when I am sick you can pick secrets out of my heart, as a child picks nut meat."

With the instinct for confession and the practice of it goes the more or less highly developed art of spiritual advice and guidance, of "direction," to use the technical Catholic phrase. As a modern psychologist expresses it: "Why should not the care of souls become an art—a system of organized and proportioned methods based upon definite knowledge of the material to be wrought upon, the ends to be attained, and the means and instruments for attaining them?" [9] This sounds a little too much like the formal procedure of the modern laboratory, which so often defeats its end by taking too great pains to achieve it. But the art of directing souls is almost as old as the world, as old as the impulse of defeat and weakness to lean upon what appears to be others' strength. There are plenty of gleams of such appeal and response in the history of Jesus and of Buddha. The whole career of Socrates, while it shows perhaps mainly an immense curiosity as to the working of men's souls, shows also a constant disposition to help them and mend them, and the relation of his disciples to him was much that of the Catholic dependents to their spiritual adviser in later centuries. The appeal of the philosopher Apollodorus to one of his followers is not unlike the appeal of Moody, though it lacks the passion: "Declare, young man, whatever good or evil you have done, so that you may obtain forgiveness by my ministry and give yourself up to philosophy with my disciples." [10] And the letters of Seneca indicate a close and careful observation, penetration, and manipulation of the souls of those who turned to him, strangely resembling the treatment administered by the doctors and artists of the Christian Church.

But it is of course under Christian belief and discipline, which set so high a value upon the individual soul and the treatment of it and the salvation of it, that the art of dealing with it has reached supreme perfection. Thousands and thousands of priests, both Catholic and Protestant, have displayed and are displaying the most delicate sympathy and the subtlest tact in guiding and advising those who turn to them for help not only in regard to the hope of another world but as to daily conduct in this. Here and there we get an illuminating glimpse of such activity; but few records are fuller or more winning than those left by the two great Catholic teachers, Francis of Sales and Fénelon. There are hundreds of letters extant, addressed by these two to their spiritual clients, and no documents give a more complete and more instructive education in the art of molding human hearts. For years these two profound and sympathetic analysts had studied the nature of those hearts, the storms that agitated them, the motives that impelled them, the advice and comfort that would relieve them, and both Fénelon and Saint Francis applied their knowledge with infinite variety and boundless success.

Sometimes it is a question of argument. The reason must be moved and enlightened. There are minds that cannot be helped and guided in any other way. "Thus we see," says Saint Francis, "that it is very natural to be subject to and guided by reasoning and opinion." And he plies such tempers with the closest logical discipline. Only, he adds with fine analysis: "melancholy people are ordinarily more attached to their opinions than those of a gay and jovial humor; for the latter are easily turned in any direction you please and are inclined to believe what one tells them." [11] Sometimes it appears that argument will not answer: some persons are not open to it or affected by it, have not the capacity for following logical trains of thought. Pure authority is needed here. Such persons must be told what to do without explanation. Or perhaps they may be puffed up with their own excellence, and a little sharp discipline or reprimand goes further than any argument. Thus Fénelon writes to one penitent: "Renounce yourself, do not love your own wit or your own courage . . . It is not even enough to relinquish oneself, one must make oneself infinitely little. Giving up is too apt to deal only with exterior things; in becoming as a little child one renounces oneself. One must learn to be little in everything and remember that one's own self counts for nothing, and one's own virtue and one's own courage for least of all." [12] And again, there are other cases in which authority, command, dictation are quite out of place, where nothing appeals or helps but tenderness, suavity, love, and in applying these ʌnd applying them rightly none before or since have ever surpassed these two great masters of the Catholic Church. With what delicate, insinuating

magic does Fénelon murmur the cardinal doctrine
without which neither he nor any other could
really and permanently bring souls to Christ: "All
the maddest passions that transport mankind are
only the true love gone astray from what should be
its eternal center. God made us to live by Him
and by His love. We were born to be both burned
and nourished by this love, as a torch is consumed
by the very light it flings abroad." [13]

And Saint Francis sums up admirably the skill,
the experience, and the natural gift required to
practice the director's art in its perfection: "Those
who govern souls must make themselves all things
to all men. In order to win all men, they must be
gentle with some, severe with others, a child with
children, a hero with heroes, a weakling with
weaklings: in short, an infinite discretion is required if one is to be fit to meet the needs of all."

III

Obviously it is subjecting Moody to a hard test
to compare him with masters of such training and
such intellectual and spiritual quality as Fénelon
and Saint Francis of Sales. Yet he comes out of
it surprisingly well. Certainly neither they nor
any one else ever had the passion for mending souls

more than he. His universal cry, "Are you a Christian?" was supplemented by the most varied and ingenious study and the most patient effort. He says that in his early years of work he established a rule: "I made it a rule that I wouldn't let a day pass without speaking to some one about their soul's salvation, and if they didn't hear the Gospel from the lips of others, there will be 365 in a year that shall hear the Gospel from my lips." [14] With such ardor you must get somewhere.

It is true that we have to recognize, perhaps most of all here, the limits that were hampering always. To deal with spirits of the quality largely handled by Fénelon and Saint Francis you have to have a somewhat different intellectual and spiritual equipment from Moody's and one can imagine persons tormented by difficulties of thought and difficulties of passion quite out of his range of experience. Sometimes also it is hard to associate such a robust physique as his with the deepest insight into the suffering of unbalanced nerves and abnormal physical organizations. Yet even in these lines he appears to have made up by intensity of sympathy what he lacked in breadth of it. That huge, solid bulk of human flesh had at times a lightness, a delicacy of spiritual touch as apt, as tender, as varied as a woman's.

And he himself was conscious of the limitations. Eager as he was, ready as he was to cast "Are you a Christian?" in every direction, he did not cast it without thought. He selected his subjects, selected the right moment for dealing with his subjects, approached them carefully, adapted his methods to the needs of the case before him. Over and over he has most admirably intelligent comments upon what he was aiming at and the care and skill necessary to obtain it. "We want to show people that we are really interested," he says. "We want to take an interest in people to show that we love them, that we desire to take them to God, and if men find that our motives are pure and that we have no selfish ends in view—why, they will believe in us." [15] He held that it was necessary to study each case as a physician studies his patients: "One may have ague, another typhoid fever, and another may have consumption. What a man wants is to be able to read his Bible and to read human nature too!" [16] He insisted constantly upon the fundamental principle in such matters, the power and the necessity of putting yourself in other people's places. Only so could you get at

their troubles and remedy them. "If we are going
to reach men, we must make them believe we are
their brothers. I will tell you how to get there.
You must put yourself in their places. I tell you,
if we only put ourselves in their places, we can
succeed in bringing souls to Christ." [17]

But beyond any definite analysis, there was unquestionably in Moody a power that took hold of
individual men, and made them over by an almost
instinctive process. I do not know any more striking illustration of this than the late President
Wilson's story of going into a barber's shop one day
where Moody was being attended to and inciden-
tally was talking to the barbers. There was nothing of cant about it, Wilson says, nothing didactic
in any way. Yet the influence was extraordinary.
"I purposely lingered in the room after he left and
noted the singular effect his visit had upon the
barbers in that shop. They talked in undertones.
They did not know his name, but they knew that
something had elevated their thought. And I felt
that I left that place as I should have left a place
of worship." [18] It may be that this man could not
have influenced the gay gallants and court ladies
with whom Fénelon dealt, though even this is by
no means certain. In any case he was the very man

283

to influence thousands of his average American fellow countrymen, like you and me.

But let us examine more in detail Moody's methods of working with souls who came to him or whom he went out to seek and of securing the conversion which was his constant and final aim. Sometimes he resorted to direct, quick, energetic argument, when he thought such argument would bowl over the last barrier and leave the Spirit free to pour itself in. A man came to him and said he could not believe. "Whom?" asked Moody. The man stammered and repeated, "I cannot believe." Again, there came the query, "Whom?" And again there was the hesitating answer, "I cannot believe, I cannot believe myself." And there flashed out the quick retort: "Well, you don't need to. You do not need to put any confidence in yourself. The less you believe in yourself the better." [19] And he pushed the doubter, and he urged him, till there seemed no refuge but the acceptance of the one solution for all his doubts. Or, there would be times when he would decline entirely to argue, when he saw that some clever logician was aching to lead him into all sorts of traps, and instead of complying he would resort to apt illustration or suggestion or emotional appeal that would make argument seem pale and out of place.

Again he felt that there were occasions when the need was rather for straight authority, when the patient was in want of discipline, or energetic control, only required to be told definitely what must be done and how it must be done. Read the striking and beautiful account of one young man who came to him with the complaint that he wanted to believe, but could not. Moody bade him turn to John 5:24 and read: "Verily, verily, I say unto you, he that heareth my word, and believeth on Him that sent me hath everlasting life." The young man read, but still hesitated. He was bidden to read it again, and yet again, and all the time, back of the bidding, was the commanding, controlling, persuading gaze and tone of the bidder, and at the end the doubts were swept away. To the gentle question, "Do you believe this?" the reply came, "Yes, indeed I do," and to the further question, "Are you a Christian?" "Yes, Mr. Moody, I am." And the convert added, in telling the story: "From that day I have never questioned my acceptance by God." [20] Sometimes in this use of authority Moody felt that he had to deal with those who were abject, despairing, to whom it seemed that there was no refuge and no escape from the black weight of sin that enveloped them. Argument had no effect. You could only insist that they must give up themselves and the thought of themselves and surrender totally to the infinite salvation. Or, on the other hand, there were those who thought themselves above the need of help, whose position in the world was so lofty or whose confidence in their own conduct was so great that it was difficult to bring them to a sense of their spiritual deficiencies at all. With these the high tone was the only tone, and no one could take it more austerely and more powerfully than Moody could. "Mr. Moody," said a lady of rank to him one day, "no one ever talked to me like this before." "Then it was quite time somebody did so," was the serene, and effective answer.[21]

In still other cases it was not a question of either argument or authority, but just of tenderness, infinite receptive comprehension of the struggles and difficulties of a sick and suffering soul. And it is in this point above all that one is sometimes astonished at the capacity of this apparently robust, hearty, almost grossly material creature to become gentle, sympathetic, tenderly responsive to every appeal and every inarticulate longing. Love was what came home to him and went out from him,

love was what touched him in the thought of
Christ and in the words of Christ, and it was
through love after all that the greatest triumphs
were to be wrought. The mightiest agency for the
conversion he was seeking was not reasoning, was
not arbitrary dictation, but the searching, uplift-
ing, dissolving, transforming potency of prayer,
and when he got his patients really to pray, he felt
that his task was done. This must not be urged
too soon. Prayer that is artificial and mechanical
does no good. "It is a good thing to get a man on
his knees (if convenient), but don't get him there
before he is ready. You may have to talk with him
two hours before you can get him that far along." [22]
But in the final conviction and transfiguration
prayer is the one medium that effects most and
most surely. And in describing the process by
which he leads to his results, he has words of a
singular, winning tenderness, which let you see
how rich he was in the varied suggestion of relief
and comfort: "In talking to an unconverted person, make it as plain as you can. Sometimes I
talk this way: ' "Come," is the first thing a mother
says to her little child. When she wants it to
learn to walk, she places it beside a chair, goes off
a little distance and then says "Come," and the

little thing lets go of the chair and runs to its mother. That is what coming means. If you can't come as a saint, come as a sinner. If you feel that your heart is so hard you are not fit to come, God wants you just as you are. He can soften your hard heart. If you are weary and heavy laden, come, and the Lord will bless you.' " [23]

IV

There are various interesting and curious phases of Moody's elaborate, long-developed, and passionate dealing with souls that well repay study. There is the question of his attack. To begin with, he centered his attention upon the will. It was the man's will that counted, that you had to mold, to bend, to break, and that once broken, the remaining barriers, whatever they might be, crumbled easily enough. As he himself puts it, "It is when the man says, 'I will.' It is the surrender of the will. The battle is fought on the will. Very often the act of getting on his knees has an effect on the man's will; but generally the will is given up before he gets there. There should be more preaching on the will." [24]

Often his methods of assailing his—victims (that word has been haunting me and finally had to come out) seem violent and abrupt. Yet there was more instinctive tact and judgment in them than might be supposed. There is the story of the man and the lamp-post. One night Moody was going home very late and it occurred to him that on that day he had not broached the great question to a single soul. He saw a perfect stranger standing under a lamp-post, and went up to him: "Are you a Christian?" The man was indignant, and Moody after a few earnest words went on his way. Weeks passed, but finally in the middle of a winter night there was a tremendous pounding on Moody's front door. Moody hurried to open, and there was the man of the lamp-post. The few words had rankled in his soul ever since, and he was determined to be saved, and he was.[25] Or there was the man with the umbrella, who took Moody under it in a hard shower. Umbrellas are useful, but had the man any shelter against the storms of hell? It seemed he had not, and his new friend was glad to furnish him with one.[26]

No doubt there were plenty of failures in the long list of varied attempts. The biographers naturally do not dwell upon these, just as the French historical painters at Versailles do not depict the French defeats. Moody himself occasionally, with characteristic frankness, brings up cases in which his best efforts were of no avail. There is the dying man, whose wife tried to save him, and Moody tried to save him, but it was no use. He was headed for hell, and it must be supposed that he went there: "My damnation is sealed, and I will be in hell in a little while." Moody labored through the last hours with passionate endeavor, but it was hopeless: "He lived a Christless life; he died a Christless death; we wrapped him in a Christless shroud, and bore him away to a Christless grave." [27] But if the failures were not unknown, and were even numerous, the list of successes is so extensive that the negative side sinks out of sight.

Moody seems to have had a remarkable gift of getting all sorts of confessions from all sorts of people. It was not that he was in the least curious or prying or anxious to entice people into the revelation of secrets which they intended to keep hid. But his large sympathy, his quick response, his faculty of making apt and helpful suggestions, drew confidences that were as abundant as they were surprising. As Dr. Abbott puts it, "Rarely, if ever, did priest, Anglican or Catholic, hear more vital confessions." [28] I think, however, that Dr.

Abbott's further comment is a little misleading. He says that "never did a High Church priest of the Anglican Church believe more profoundly that to him had been given authority to promise the absolution and remission of sins than did Mr. Moody believe that he possessed such authority." [29] It is true that Moody felt perfectly competent to assure his penitents that salvation could be obtained and to tell them how it could be obtained. But I do not think he ever professed to grant it to them. On the contrary, he was careful to emphasize that everything depended on the sinner himself, and he declares explicitly against any definite assurance from without. When asked if he would tell inquirers that they were saved, he replied: "No, let God tell them. That record is kept on high. I think it is very wrong to tell inquirers they are saved. They can be saved by putting their trust in the Lord God in Heaven." [30] He was far too wise, too shrewd, to pretend that any human being can take upon himself the entire burden of the soul of another.

A most interesting aspect of this confession side of Moody's work is his relations with women. We have seen before that he was anything but a woman's man. Indeed, it is very striking how pe-

culiarly powerful his influence was with men. The
great Catholic confessors I have referred to above
largely dealt with women, and their hold upon
men seems to have been much less substantial; but
the men flocked to Moody and he had the secret of
touching them by his infinite manliness. In his
excellent advice as to dealing with inquiring souls
he insists upon the wisdom of keeping out of sex
complications: "Don't take those in a position in
life above your own, but as a rule, take those on
the same footing. Don't deal with a person of the
opposite sex, if it can be otherwise arranged." [31]
He would no doubt readily have endorsed the advice of the Imitation: "Be not a friend to any one
woman in particular, but commend all good women in general to God." His infinite practical
skill and tact showed themselves occasionally in
dealing with those situations in which scheming
women endeavor to take advantage of ministerial
simplicity and candor.[32] And never in one single
instance did the slightest taint of reproach or
scandal attach itself to him, even from his bitterest
critics.

Yet he had a profound admiration and respect
for women and used their advice and assistance in
ways which a Catholic priest could hardly have

accepted. He never indulges in such mild sarcasm about them as Saint Jerome's, "What shall we do with these wretched little women, saturated with petty sins, who veer with every breeze of doctrine, who are always asking questions, and never learn anything from the answers?" [33] or even that of the gentle Saint Francis, "To tell the truth, the sex is marvelously inclined to pity themselves and to expect others to pity them." [34] We have seen Moody's high opinion of his wife's gift at conversion, and he felt that women generally could do things in that line that men could not. Also, as you look through his sermons you find many interesting and curious cases in which women evidently came to him about their deepest secrets and received help and comfort even as did the men. And the sermon especially addressed to fallen women is well worth consideration for tact and dignity in dealing with a difficult subject. [35]

Another important phase of Moody's work with souls is the intensely practical side of it. He was determined that those whom he helped should not only feel salvation but should live it: "Christianity isn't worth a snap of your finger if it doesn't straighten out your characters. I have got tired of all your mere gush and sentiment." [36] Life was to be made over, not only inwardly but outwardly, and the spiritual grace was to show everywhere and always in the practical conduct. Fundamental as faith was, works were the crowning glory of it.

He did not indeed insist upon penance in the Catholic sense, the difficult and dangerous doctrine that later self-inflicted discomfort can make up for earlier sin. But he did demand, as an essential preliminary to any claim upon the Kingdom of Heaven, not only that there should be profound repentence and regret for past misdoing, but that wrong that had been done should be remedied so far as possible. He recounts some extraordinary cases of men and women who had come to him declaring their passionate desire to be reconciled with God, but admitting that in the past they had done some one a wrong which they were unwilling or thought themselves unable to remedy. With such people his insistence was iron. Restitution, reparation, must be made, before he would have anything to do with them. Sometimes, to be sure, he recognizes the infinite bitterness of the struggle, sometimes confesses frankly how hard it would be for himself to meet it. But it has to be met, all the same. Only so can there be any assurance that God will forgive and accept.

And again, there is bitterness, enmity, hard feeling. If people are to find salvation under his guidance, there must be absolute forgiveness, no cherishing of grudges, no putting them on one side and conveniently burying them. There must be open reconciliation and penitence coming obviously and full from the heart. He gives interesting illustrations of this, most often with women, as in the case of the young ladies, who were eager to be set right, but could not possibly get over their dislike to each other. They got over it, under Moody's insistence: "It so happened that they started about the same time to ask each other's forgiveness. They met in the middle of the room, one of the most joyous meetings I ever witnessed, threw their arms around each other, and both speaking at the same time, said, 'I want you to forgive me.' The Lord met them right there." [37] On the other hand, there is the lamentable case of the woman who would never forgive: if that was essential, she would never become a Christian. "And the last I heard of her she had gone out of her mind, and some infidels say religion drove her out of her mind, but it was the want of it, that is what it was." [38]

One element of the work of the great Catholic

directors I miss in Moody, that is the element of continued guidance. He was no letter writer, and he was too busy to write letters any way. When the first stroke was achieved, he necessarily passed on, to convert thousands more. The steady, daily pressure had in most cases to be left to others. At the same time, this does not mean that his work was not permanent in a vast number of cases. Again and again we read of those who had been converted by him coming to him in later years and expressing their steadfast hold upon the supreme gift that he had given them, and I do not know how there could be a finer statement of this permanence than the remark of Drummond: "I have never heard him quoted as a theologian. But I know of large numbers of men and women of all churches and creeds, of many countries and ranks, from the poorest to the richest, and from the most ignorant to the most wise, upon whom he has placed an ineffaceable moral mark." [39]

It is needless to enlarge upon the delight that came to converter, as well as to converted, when these spiritual miracles were performed. To a heart eager and passionate as Moody's, the development of life and light and ecstasy in each new case of salvation was almost like repeating your

ROUND TOP : THE BURIAL PLACE.

A place especially sacred to Mr. Moody during his lifetime.

1837   1899

The Autobiography of DWIGHT L. MOODY

SOME day you will read in the papers that D. L. Moody, of East Northfield, is dead. Don't you believe a word of it! At that moment I shall be more alive than I am now. I shall have gone up higher, that is all; out of this old clay tenement into a house that is immortal—a body that death cannot touch; that sin cannot taint; a body fashioned like unto His glorious body.

I was born of the flesh in 1837. I was born of the Spirit in 1856. That which is born of the flesh may die. That which is born of the Spirit will live forever.

own salvation over and over. I do not know how I can better illustrate the whole process that the newly regenerate went through than by quoting the long account given by one subject who had traversed it from beginning to end: "I went to hear him speak out of curiosity at first. After a while I began to feel troubled in my mind. Then I grew irritated, when I fancied that he had singled me out and was talking at me, pointing out my sins and asking me to repent. I didn't like it. I wanted him to leave me alone. I didn't dare to look up for fear that every one in the church was looking at me with pity. If I had been near the door, I would have slipped out. I wondered how he had found out all the little mean things I had ever done. Then I began to grow ashamed of myself, tried not to listen to what he was saying. But he kept right on talking to me. He paid no attention to anybody else there, though I knew some of them were worse than I was—and all the time I was growing more sorry and ashamed. Then all at once he stopped talking and asked everybody to sing. They sang, 'What a Friend We Have in Jesus,' and it seemed to lift me right out of my seat and carry me down the aisle; and I couldn't stop till I was on my knees in front of the platform, with the tears running down my face. . . . He took my hand in his and told me that if I felt convicted of my sins and just surrendered completely to the Lord Jesus Christ, I would be saved. I asked him how I could feel sure of salvation, what evidence I had. He looked at me for a moment in that gentle way—as only Moody could look. 'Your own soul tells you that,' he said tenderly and sympathetically. It was a supreme moment of my life." [40] As it would surely be of any one's.

V

So we see that Moody enjoyed three of the intensest excitements and intoxications known to man: that of stirring a vast audience by his own unaided power, that of moving men to do his bidding in the practical affairs of this world, and that of saving souls; but of the three the latter, though perhaps not the most immediately intense, is assuredly the most varied and the most enduring. And again, as with the other intoxicants, there is always the danger that such power will turn a man's head, will make him arrogant and unduly arbitrary in his dealings with others. How immense the power is appears admirably in the comment of Henry Ward Beecher upon it: "I am ashamed of myself positively to be an object of more faith than my Savior; yet I have persons coming to me every day of my life with their wants and troubles, and when I think of the injustice of coming to me thus instead of going to Christ, I feel just like pushing them away. How eagerly they believe every statement I make; how they hang upon my sympathy and hope I will let them come again tomorrow." [41] It is safe to say that Moody was quite as much haunted by such persons as Beecher was. Yet there is no evidence whatever that his head was turned or that in his later years he treated them with any less humility or self-forgetfulness than in his youth. But he did enjoy it. There is no denying that. Neither Beecher nor any one else could emphasize the power more clearly than he does: "The longer I live the more I am convinced it is a greater thing to influence a man's will; a man whose will is set against God; to have that will broken and brought into subjection to God's will—or, in other words, it is a greater thing to have power over a living, sinning, God-hating man, than to quicken the dead." [42] And he reveled to the full in the exercise of it: "Then the joy of winning men to Christ. There is no joy like it. I thought when I was converted that

that was a great joy, but, oh, the bliss of saving others. There is no joy in the world like that. The luxury of winning a soul to Christ, the luxury of being used by God in building up his kingdom, the luxury of hearing the young convert testify of what God has done for him." [43] Or, as he sums it up elsewhere: "It is the greatest pleasure of living to win souls to Christ, and it is a pleasure that Angels can't enjoy." [44]

The excitement, the exaltation, were so great that he liked to think that there were no limits to his power, that is, to the power of God working in him. Only go at it right, he says, and you can accomplish all things: "I have hardly ever known in my life a man who resented being spoken to about his soul. Of course you must go the right way to work and wait for the guiding of the Spirit. But in 999 cases out of a thousand a wise, skillful conversation on the deepest things of the soul is not resented." [45] At another time, referring to a hard subject who had been conquered, he puts it even more sweepingly and universally: "In all my acquaintances I don't know of a man whom it seemed more hopeless to reach. I believe if we lay ourselves out for the work, there is not a man in Boston"—and surely impossibility could go no further than Boston—"but can be reached and saved. I don't care who he is, if we go in the name of our Master, and persevere till we succeed." [46]

What a delicious range of conjectures does this passage open. Constantly, as I have followed Moody's triumphant course of effort and success, I have thought to myself of the innumerable types whom it seemed to me impossible that he could have influenced by any ingenuity whatever, and I have set down little imaginary dialogues in which his insistent "Are you a Christian?" received the greatest variety of answers. The hardened children of this world are perhaps more easily reached than might be supposed. Their indifference and disregard are sometimes melted, if you can once call their attention to matters they have deliberately thrust on one side. But there are more subtle, thoughtful tempers whom Moody could surely never have touched. I have already referred to a conceivable confrontation with Lincoln. What could he have made of Goethe, or of Shelley, or of Flaubert? Every one of them would have been courteous, would have been interested. But his skillful conversation on the deepest things of the soul would have fallen off them like snow-flakes that melt before they can be noticed.

I think he would have had most trouble with those that were most like himself and those that were least. Mr. Duffus has excellently pointed out with what astonishment, indignation, and resentment Moody would have met any one who had assailed him with the certainly very appropriate query, "Are you a Christian?" On the other hand, let us take our Shakespearean clown, who, as I have said before, has no soul, or all soul, whose own fluid personality is lost, dissolved, in the quick, gracious play of the mobile world about him. When Moody assails him with the eternal interrogatory can you not imagine his answer: "No, no, Moody, I am too little. And, Moody, let me warn you that that vast, swollen, humble, eternal consequence of yours is filling the whole infinite universe, and light and gayety and laughter and even God are being crowded into a little wee corner. If you don't take care, they will be crowded out altogether, and your vast consequence, and all this sun-warmed, wind-swept, laughter-lighted universe will turn to nothing." And the clown would go his way, and Moody his.

Yet, though there were so many upon whom Moody could have made no impression, upon whom, with his keen practical sense, he would never have attempted to make any, we must remember how many thousands there were who needed his help, whom he could help, and whom he did help.

That is all, I think. And the question finally arises, whether the doctrines that Moody preached will fade and vanish, or whether with a strange and indestructible vitality they will survive, in one form or another, to move the world. Surely we may end as we began, with the insistence that God is the one supreme universal need of all humanity, and that that need was never more pronounced than in America to-day. Not long ago a brilliant and popular author, who would certainly never be associated with evangelistic propaganda, wrote me in regard to a review of one of his books: "What I really want to thank you for is your perception that I am interested in nothing else in the world, seriously, except speculations and wonderings about God . . . I suppose, if we would all admit it, none of us is really interested in anything else." It makes no difference how you define God. You need not define Him at all, but fall back upon the saying of Emerson, "In your metaphysics you have denied personality to the Deity, yet when the devout motions of the Soul come, yield to them heart and life, though they should clothe God with shape and color." [47] The simple fact is, that, if God does not exist, the universe is but a wilderness of barren horror. If He does exist, life should be but one long effort to know Him and be at one with Him. Separation from Him is the most terrible punishment the mind can conceive. As one of the very greatest of English prose writers expresses it: "What Tophet is not Paradise, what brimstone is not amber, what gnashing is not a comfort, what gnawing of the worm is not a tickling, what torment is not a marriage-bed to this damnation, to be secluded eternally, eternally, eternally from the sight of God?" [48]

It may be that in the future others will have different ways of overcoming this separation from those that appealed to D. L. Moody. But it will not be denied that in his day none worked more passionately, more lovingly, and more successfully to bring God to man and man to God.

BOOKS BY D. L. MOODY. THE TITLES IN
ITALICS ARE THOSE USED FOR REFERENCE
IN THE NOTES

Bible Characters, Revell, 1888.
Glad Tidings, E. B. Treat, 1876.
Heaven, Revell, 1880.
Latest Sermons, Colportage Association, 1900.
Life and Sermons, J. S. Ogilvie, 1900.
Men of the Bible, Colportage Association, 1898.
The Overcoming Life, Revell, 1896.
Pleasure and Profit in Bible Study, Revell, 1895.
Prevailing Prayer, Revell, 1885.
Secret Power, Revell, 1881.
Select Sermons, Colportage Association, no date.
Short Talks, Colportage Association, 1900.
Sowing and Reaping, Revell, 1896.
Moody's *Stories,* Colportage Association, 1899.
To All People, E. B. Treat, 1877.
To the Work, Revell, 1896.
The Way Home, Colportage Association, 1904.
Weighed and Found Wanting, Colportage Association, 1898.

BOOKS BIOGRAPHICAL AND CRITICAL, WITH THE ABBREVIATIONS USED IN REFERRING TO THEM IN THE NOTES

Abbott, Lyman, *Silhouettes of My Contemporaries.*   Abbott, *Silhouettes.*

Begbie, Harold, *Life of William Booth.*   Begbie, *Booth.*

Beardsley, Frank Grenville, *A History of American Revivals.*   Beardsley.

Biederwolf, William E., *Evangelism.*   Biederwolf.

Chapman, J. Wilbur, *The Life and Work of Dwight L. Moody.*   Chapman.

Clark, Rufus W., *The Great Work of God in Great Britain under Messrs. Moody and Sankey.*   Clark.

Coe, George A., *The Spiritual Life.*   Coe.

Conant, William C., *Narratives of Remarkable Conversions and Revival Incidents.*   Conant.

Cumming, I. A. M., *Tabernacle Sketches.*   *Tabernacle Sketches.*

Daniels, Reverend W. H., *D. L. Moody and His Work.*   Daniels, *D. L. Moody.*

Daniels, W. H., *Moody: His Words, Work, and Workers.*   Daniels, *Moody.*

Dewey, Orville, *Letters of an English Traveler to His Friend in England on the Revivals of Religion.*   Dewey.

Duffus, Robert L., *The Hound of Heaven,* in *American Mercury,* April, 1925, vol. v, pp. 424-432.

Farwell, John V., *Early Recollections of Dwight L. Moody.*   Farwell.

BIOGRAPHICAL BOOKS

Finney, Reverend Charles G., *Memoirs, Written by Himself.*
Finney, *Memoirs.*

Goodspeed, Reverend E. J., *A Full History of the Wonderful Career of Moody and Sankey in Great Britain and America.*
Goodspeed.

Goss, Charles F., *Echoes from the Pulpit and Platform.*
Goss.

Hall, John, and George H. Stuart, *The American Evangelists, D. L. Moody and Ira D. Sankey in Great Britain and Ireland.*
Hall.

James, William, *The Varieties of Religious Experience.*
James, *Varieties.*

Kernahan, A. Earl, *Visitation Evangelism.*
Kernahan.

McDowell, John, *Dwight L. Moody.*
McDowell.

Moody, Paul D. and A. P. Fitt, *The Shorter Life of D. L. Moody.*
Paul Moody.

Moody, W. R., *The Life of Dwight L. Moody.*
Moody, D. L., at Home.
W. R. Moody.
Moody at Home.

Nason, Reverend Elias, *The American Evangelists Dwight L. Moody and Ira D. Sankey.*
Nason.

Northrop, Henry Davenport, *Life and Labors of Dwight L. Moody.*
Northrop.

Pascal, Blaise, *Pensées,* (édition Louandre).
Pascal, *Pensées.*

Sainte-Beuve, C. A., *Port-Royal.*
Sainte-Beuve, *Port-Royal.*

Sales, Saint Francis of, *Œuvres,* (edition 1833).
Saint Francis, *Œuvres.*

Sankey, Ira D., *My Life and the Story of the Gospel Songs.*
Sankey.

Stebbins, George C., *Reminiscences, and Gospel Hymn Stories.*
Stebbins.

Torrey, R. A., *Why God Used D. L. Moody.* — Torrey.

Tracy, Joseph, *The Great Awakening.* — Tracy.

Tyerman, Reverend L., *The Life and Times of Reverend John Wesley.* — Tyerman.

Underwood, Alfred Clair, *Conversion, Christian and Non-Christian.* — Underwood.

Willard, Frances E., *Glimpses of Fifty Years.* — Willard, *Glimpses.*

Williamson, David, *Ira. D. Sankey.* — Williamson.

NOTES

CHAPTER I: THE GROWTH OF A SOUL

1. *Short Talks,* p. 100.
2. Duffus, p. 424.
3. Willard, *Glimpses,* p. 633.
4. Daniels, *D. L. Moody,* p. 13.
5. *Stories,* p. 80.
6. W. R. Moody, p. 24.
7. *Weighed and Found Wanting,* p. 53.
8. *Stories,* p. 106.
9. Nason, p. 31.
10. *Glad Tidings,* p. 69.
11. *The Way Home,* p. 41.
12. *Glad Tidings,* p. 164.
13. Cumming, p. 81.
14. *Latest Sermons,* p. 120.
15. Goss, p. 84.
16. *Glad Tidings,* p. 456.
17. *Boston Advertiser,* March 31, 1877.
18. Goss, p. 39.
19. Daniels, *D. L. Moody,* p. 51.
20. Id., p. 54.
21. Id., p. 190.
22. Goss, p. 48.
23. *Short Talks,* p. 79.
24. Darwin to Henslow, April 1, 1848, *More Letters of Charles Darwin,* vol. i, p. 61.
25. Begbie, *Booth,* vol. i, p. 225.
26. Sermon in *Boston Transcript,* February, 1, 1877.
27. *Tabernacle Sketches,* p. 12.
28. *Glad Tidings,* p. 452.
29. *Prevailing Prayer,* p. 51.
30. *Heaven,* p. 8.
31. Underwood, *Conversion,* p. 11.

32. Finney, *Memoirs,* p. 263.
33. Finney, *Memoirs,* p. 20.
34. Harold Begbie, *Twice-born Men,* p. 204.
35. Underwood, *Conversion,* p. 223.
36. Jonathan Edwards, *A Narrative of Conversions,* section iii.
37. *Short Talks,* p. 78.
38. *Pleasure and Profit,* p. 91.
39. W. R. Moody, p. 42.
40. *Men of the Bible,* p. 23.
41. Torrey, p. 53.
42. Sermon, in *Boston Advertiser,* February 1, 1877.
43. Northrop, p. 528.
44. Torrey, p. 9.
45. *Life and Sermons,* p. 353.
46. *To All People,* p. 164.
47. Northrop, p. 79.
48. Daniels, *D. L. Moody,* p. 116.
49. *To All People,* p. 168.
50. Goss, p. 40.
51. Daniels, *D. L. Moody,* p. 149.

CHAPTER II: HEAVEN AND HELL

1. Pascal, *Pensées,* I.
2. Goodspeed, p. 315.
3. *Heaven,* p. 8.
4. Kelman, in Daniels, *D. L. Moody,* p. 269.
5. *Pleasure and Profit,* p. 20.
6. *Pleasure and Profit,* p. 26.
7. *To All People,* p. 508.
8. Goss, p. 104.
9. *Life and Sermons,* p. 191.
10. *Stories,* p. 55.
11. *Tabernacle Sketches,* preface.
12. *Tabernacle Sketches,* p. 38.
13. *Heaven,* p. 9.
14. *Prevailing Prayer,* p. 77.
15. *Latest Sermons,* p. 53.
16. *Secret Power,* p. 76.

NOTES

17. Underwood, p. 106.
18. John Dyer, in *Penn Monthly*, June, 1875, vol. vi, p. 430.
19. Dewey, p. 19.
20. In *Harper's Magazine*, November, 1917, vol. cxxxv, p. 858.
21. See Edward Hitchcock, *Life of Mary Lyon*, p. 155.
22. *Oldtown Folks* (Riverside edition), vol. ii, p. 54.
23. Finney, *Memoirs*, p. 104.
24. Begbie, *Booth*, vol i, p. 412.
25. Dewey, p. 64.
26. Quoted in Tracy, p. 215.
27. Conant, p. 43.
28. In Beardsley, p. 270.
29. *Thoughts on the Revival*, section v.
30. *Maximen und Reflexionen*, section iii.
31. *Thoughts on the Revival*, section v.
32. St. John of the Cross, in James, *Varieties*, p. 306.
33. Arthur Schopenhauer, *The World as Will and Idea* (translation Haldane and Kemp), vol. i, p. 532.
34. *The Way Home*, p. 12.
35. *The Way Home*, p. 81.
36. *Silhouettes*, p. 201.
37. Saint Teresa, *The Way of Perfection* (translation by the Benedictines of Stanbrook), p. 174.
38. Sénancour, *Obermann*, p. 40.
39. *The Way Home*, p. 68.
40. Quoted by James H. Leuba, *Studies in the Psychology of Religious Phenomena*, *American Journal of Psychology*, April, 1896, vol. vii, p. 324.
41. *Pensées*, xxiv, 35.
42. John Morley, *Critical Miscellanies*, vol. i. p. 344.
43. Quoted in *Outlook*, September 26, 1908, vol. xc, p. 175.
44. *Weighed and Found Wanting*, p. 121.
45. *Short Talks*, p. 76.
46. Finney, *Memoirs*, p. 171.
47. *Select Sermons*, p. 45.
48. Madame Du Deffand to Voltaire, February 28, 1766, Voltaire, *Correspondance*, vol. xii, p. 231.
49. In James, *Varieties*, p. 137. As Dr. A. W. Vernon points

out to me, this is taken from Eckermann, *Gespräche Mit Goethe,* January 27, 1824, vol. i, p. 76.

50. *To All People,* p. 162.
51. Jean Jacques Brousson, *Anatole France Himself* (translation Pollock), p. 70.
52. *Short Talks,* p. 90.
53. James, *Varieties,* p. 47.

CHAPTER III: MOODY THE PREACHER

1. John Dyer, in *Penn Monthly,* June, 1875, vol. vi, p. 433.
2. *Ibid.*
3. Finney, *Memoirs,* p. 81.
4. *Men of the Bible,* p. 32.
5. Whitefield's *Diary,* in Tracy, p. 107.
6. Nason, p. 85.
7. *Saturday Review,* March 13, 1875, vol. xxxix, p. 344.
8. *Silhouettes,* p. 200.
9. *Tabernacle Sketches,* p. 12.
10. Goss, p. 96.
11. *To All People,* p. 179.
12. *The Overcoming Life,* p. 72.
13. W. R. Moody, p. 441.
14. W. R. Moody, p. 459.
15. Torrey, p. 24.
16. Dr. Joseph Collins, in *Harper's Magazine,* November, 1917, vol. cxxxv, p. 864.
17. W. R. Moody, p. 315.
18. *Silhouettes,* p. 200.
19. W. R. Moody, p. 500.
20. W. R. Moody, p. 509.
21. Goodspeed, p. 238.
22. Goss, p. 101.
23. *To All People,* p. 185.
24. Clara Erskine Clement, *Charlotte Cushman,* p. 100.
25. *Ramakrishna, His Life and Sayings,* in James, *Varieties,* p. 365.
26. *Port-Royal,* vol. i, p. 268.
27. Begbie, *Booth,* vol. i, p. 88.

NOTES

28. Begbie, *Booth,* vol. i, p. 47.
29. *Pensées,* iii, 2.
30. *Confessions,* book x, chapter 37.
31. Tyerman, vol. ii, p. 595.
32. *Ibid.*
33. Reverend Jonathan Parsons, of revival in Lynn, Connecticut, 1741, in Tracy, p. 139.
34. Finney, *Memoirs,* p. 228.
35. James Stalker, in *Sunday Magazine,* reprinted in *Living Age,* May 24, 1900, vol. lxx, p. 398.
36. *Life and Sermons,* p. 140.
37. *The Overcoming Life,* p. 83.
38. *Glad Tidings,* p. 471.
39. Torrey, p. 28.
40. Duffus, p. 429.
41. Conant, p. 24.
42. *Life and Sermons,* p. 87.
43. *Life and Sermons,* p. 81.
44. Chapman, p. 276.
45. Nason, p. 59.
46. *Glad Tidings,* p. 375.
47. Nason, p. 82.
48. Robert Burton, *Anatomy of Melancholy,* part ii, section 2, member 3.
49. Tracy, p. 427.
50. Clark, p. 34.
51. W. R. Moody, p. 360.
52. *Life and Sermons,* p. 110.
53. W. R. Moody, p. 2.
54. *Moody at Home,* p. 29.
55. Dewey, p. 12.
56. *To All People,* p. 425.
57. *Weighed and Found Wanting,* p. 47.
58. *Latest Sermons,* p. 58.
59. *Weighed and Found Wanting,* p. 59.
60. Richard Whiteing, in *Manchester Guardian,* reprinted in *Living Age,* September 30, 1919, vol. cccii, p. 734.

D. L. MOODY: A WORKER IN SOULS

CHAPTER IV: MOODY AND SANKEY

1. Williamson, p. 37.
2. Duffus, p. 428.
3. Goodspeed, p. 539.
4. A. C. Benson, in Underwood, p. 208.
5. Nason, p. 234.
6. January 29, 1877.
7. W. R. Moody, p. 174.
8. Williamson, p. 145.
9. Daniels, *D. L. Moody,* p. 230.
10. Hall, p. 18.
11. Williamson, p. 121.
12. Goodspeed, p. 280.
13. Hall, p. 79.
14. Sankey, p. 80.
15. *Tabernacle Sketches,* p. 32.
16. Williamson, p. 12.
17. Sankey, p. 13.
18. Williamson, p. 154.
19. Nason, p. 235.
20. Williamson, p. 45. Also, in Sankey, pp. 305-307.
21. Goodspeed, p. 580.
22. Williamson, p. 21, and in many other places, with the usual variants.
23. Northrop, p. 86.
24. W. R. Moody, p. 180.
25. Williamson, p. 49.
26. Northrop, p. 176.
27. Goodspeed, p. 539.
28. Northrop, p. 210.
29. Sankey, p. 70.
30. *Glad Tidings,* p. 449.
31. Goodspeed, p. 582.
32. W. R. Moody, p. 259.
33. Northrop, p. 517.
34. Northrop, p. 176.
35. Goodspeed, p. 589.
36. *To All People,* p. 424.

NOTES

37. Goss, p. 53.
38. W. R. Moody, p. 529.
39. Underwood, p. 207.
40. Preface to *Dawn Boy,* by Edna Lou Walton.
41. Tyerman, vol. i, p. 398.
42. *Secret Power,* p. 118.
43. *To All People,* p. 171.
44. *Stories,* p. 46.
45. Northrop, p. 535.
46. Goss, p. 100.
47. *Tabernacle Sketches,* p. 11.
48. E. F. Rimbault, in *Leisure Hour,* 1875, vol. xxiv, p. 476.
49. Clark, p. 51.
50. Goodspeed, p. 294.
51. In Underwood, p. 208.
52. Clark, p. 51.
53. Printed at length in *My Life and the Story of the Gospel Songs.*
54. Clark, p. 49.
55. *The World Soul.*
56. *Essay on Love, Essays, First Series,* p. 84 (Riverside edition, 1884).
57. Cowper to Newton, September 9, 1781, Cowper's *Correspondence* (edition Wright), vol. i, p. 351.
58. Quoted by E. F. Rimbault, in *Leisure Hour,* 1875, vol. xxiv, p. 475.

CHAPTER V: MOODY THE MAN

1. *Glad Tidings,* p. 490.
2. Scotch Journalist, in Hall, p. 189.
3. Nason, p. 77.
4. W. R. Moody, p. 553.
5. Goss, p. 83.
6. Northrop, p. 188.
7. Sermon in *Boston Advertiser,* January 30, 1877.
8. Daniels, *Moody,* p. 473.
9. Quoted in *Outlook,* December 30, 1899, vol. lxiii, p. 998.
10. In Abbott, *Silhouettes,* p. 206.

D. L. MOODY: A WORKER IN SOULS

11. *Life and Sermons,* p. 154.
12. W. R. Moody, p. 552.
13. *Life and Sermons,* p. 194.
14. *Select Sermons,* p. 67.
15. Torrey, p. 33.
16. Torrey, p. 36.
17. Nason, p. 80.
18. Farwell, p. 81.
19. W. R. Moody, p. 589.
20. *The Overcoming Life,* p. 16.
21. Goss, p. 86.
22. Goss, p. 85.
23. Clark, p. 36.
24. Chapman, p. 26.
25. Stebbins, p. 313.
26. Goss, p. 63.
27. Goodspeed, p. 587.
28. W. R. Moody, p. 38.
29. W. R. Moody, p. 30.
30. Paul Moody, p. 24.
31. Stebbins, p. 314.
32. W. R. Moody, p. 518.
33. *Secret Power,* p. 122.
34. James, *Varieties,* p. 365.
35. Daniels, *D. L. Moody,* p. 30.
36. Williamson, p. 154.
37. Northrop, p. 461.
38. Pascal, *Pensées,* xxiv, 60.
39. *Latest Sermons,* p. 53.
40. W. R. Moody, p. 517.
41. W. R. Moody, p. 23.
42. Paul Moody, p. 95.
43. W. R. Moody, p. 523.
44. *The Overcoming Life,* p. 30.
45. Nason, p. 51.
46. W. R. Moody, p. 507.
47. *Men of the Bible,* p. 56.
48. *Glad Tidings,* p. 150.

NOTES

49. *Life and Sermons,* p. 320.
50. Willard, *Glimpses,* p. 361.
51. Daniels, *D. L. Moody,* p. 94.
52. *Glad Tidings,* p. 328.
53. *Life and Sermons,* p. 173.
54. *Short Talks,* p. 77.
55. Sainte-Beuve, *Port-Royal,* vol. i, p. 359.
56. *To All People,* p. 39.
57. Nason, p. 345.
58. Goodspeed, p. 234.
59. Episcopal Clergyman, in *Independent,* March 5, 1903, vol. lv, p. 538.

CHAPTER VI: MOODY THE MAN OF BUSINESS

1. Goss, p. 53.
2. W. R. Moody, p. 509.
3. *Ibid.*
4. *Moody at Home,* p. 112.
5. McDowell, p. 56.
6. Stebbins, p. 207.
7. *Tabernacle Sketches,* p. 11.
8. *Life and Sermons,* p. 48.
9. Torrey, p. 24.
10. Goss, p. 91.
11. McDowell, p. 54.
12. W. R. Moody, p. 46.
13. Paul Moody, p. 95.
14. Duffus, p. 429.
15. In *Outlook,* January 20, 1900, vol. lxiv, p. 164.
16. Tracy, p. 258.
17. Goss, p. 85.
18. Northrop, p. 517.
19. To the Perronets, Tyerman, vol. ii, p. 85.
20. Begbie, *Booth,* vol. i, p. 427.
21. Finney, p. 192.
22. Nason, p. 83.
23. W. R. Moody, p. 180.
24. Torrey, p. 8.

25. *Men of the Bible,* p. 24.
26. *Men of the Bible,* p. 7.
27. *Lettres Spirituelles,* No. 40.
28. *To the Work,* p. 32.
29. *Glad Tidings,* p. 58.
30. Willard, *Glimpses,* p. 358.
31. Daniels, *D. L. Moody,* p. 28.
32. Daniels, *D. L. Moody,* p. 29.
33. W. R. Moody, p. 263.
34. Begbie, *Booth,* vol. i, p. 384.
35. Northrop, p. 77.
36. Daniels, *D. L. Moody,* p. 127.
37. Torrey, p. 15.
38. Goss, p. 67.
39. Daniels, *D. L. Moody,* p. 171.
40. W. R. Moody, p. 457.
41. *Tabernacle Sketches,* p. 12.
42. *Unitarian Review, Editor's Note Book,* March, 1877.
43. *To All People,* p. 169.
44. *To All People,* p. 181.
45. Goss, p. 4.
46. *Latest Sermons,* p. 111.
47. Goss, p. 90.
48. *Ibid.*
49. *Glad Tidings,* p. 14.
50. Dr. Henry F. Cutler, in McDowell, p. 44.
51. Beth Bradford Gilchrist, *The Life of Mary Lyon,* p. 198.

CHAPTER VII: THE MOLDER OF SOULS

1. Duffus, p. 430.
2. Finney, *Memoirs,* p. 92.
3. Dewey, p. 56.
4. *Saturday Review,* May 22, 1875, vol. xxxix, p. 656.
5. *Moody at Home,* p. 41.
6. *Moody at Home,* p. 73.
7. Coe, p. 56.
8. Quoted in Henry Charles Lea, *A History of Auricular Confession,* vol. ii, p. 456.

NOTES

9. Coe, p. 21.
10. Quoted in C. P. de Lasteyrie, *The History of Auricular Confession* (translation), vol. i, p. 59.
11. Saint Francis of Sales, *Œuvres,* vol. iv, p. 217.
12. In Jules Lemaitre, *Fénelon,* p. 262.
13. *Lettres Spirituelles, in Œuvres Choisies* (edition Hachette, 1910), vol. iv, p. 114.
14. *Glad Tidings,* p. 52.
15. *To All People,* p. 75.
16. *Pleasure and Profit,* p. 117.
17. *Glad Tidings,* p. 63.
18. McDowell, p. 39.
19. *Select Sermons,* p. 120.
20. Beardsley, p. 322.
21. W. R. Moody, p. 392.
22. *Pleasure and Profit,* p. 120.
23. *Moody at Home,* p. 50.
24. *Moody at Home,* p. 70.
25. Torrey, p. 39.
26. Torrey, p. 43.
27. *Glad Tidings,* p, 261.
28. In *North American Review,* February, 1900, vol. clxx, p. 270.
29. *Ibid.*
30. *To All People,* p. 176.
31. *Pleasure and Profit,* p. 121.
32. Farwell, p. 28.
33. Epistles of Saint Jerome, No. 133, freely translated from the French of Gaston Boissier, in *La Fin du Paganisme,* vol. ii, p. 81.
34. *Œuvres,* vol. xi, p. 288.
35. In Daniels, *Moody,* pp. 334-441.
36. *Life and Sermons,* p. 313.
37. *To All People,* p. 126.
38. *To All People,* p. 124.
39. In Chapman, p. 31.
40. Article on Moody's Northfield Home, in *National Magazine,* February, 1900, vol. xi, p. 478.

41. Address by Beecher, in Conant, p. 383.
42. *Stories,* p. 66.
43. Sermon, in *Boston Transcript,* February 1, 1877.
44. *Glad Tidings,* p. 51.
45. Williamson, p. 105.
46. *To All People,* p. 162.
47. *Essays, first series* (Riverside edition, 1884), p. 58.
48. Sermon of John Donne, in Bullen's edition of the *Works of John Marston,* vol. i, p. lx.